EXCITING
EXTRA
ONLINE
RESOURCES
INCLUDED

D0654285

Kaplan Publishing are constantly finding new ways to make a difference to your studies and our exciting online resources really do offer something different to AAT students looking for exam success.

FOR THE FIRST TIME, KAPLAN'S AAT TEXTS COME WITH FREE EN-gage ONLINE RESOURCES SO THAT YOU CAN STUDY ANYTIME, ANYWHERE

Having purchased this Kaplan Text, you have access to the following online study materials:

AH1299

- An online version of the Text
- Fixed Online Tests with instant answers

How to access your online resources

- **Kaplan Financial students** will already have a Kaplan EN-gage account and these extra resources will be available to you online. You do not need to register again, as this process was completed when you enrolled. If you are having problems accessing online materials, please ask your course administrator.
- **If you purchased through Kaplan Flexible Learning or via the Kaplan Publishing website** you will automatically receive an e-mail invitation to Kaplan EN-gage online. Please register your details using this e-mail to gain access to your content. If you do not receive the e-mail or book content, please contact Kaplan Flexible Learning.
- **If you are already a registered Kaplan EN-gage user** go to www.EN-gage.co.uk and log in. Select the 'add a book' feature and enter the ISBN number of this book and the unique pass key at the bottom of this card. Then click 'finished' or 'add another book'. You may add as many books as you have purchased from this screen.
- **If you are a new Kaplan EN-gage user** register at www.EN-gage.co.uk and click on the link contained in the e-mail we sent you to activate your account. Then select the 'add a book' feature, enter the ISBN number of this book and the unique pass key at the bottom of this card. Then click 'finished' or 'add another book'.

Your Code and Information

This code can only be used once for the registration of one book online. This registration will expire when the final sittings for the examinations covered by this book have taken place. Please allow one hour from the time you submitted your book details for us to process your request.

Please scratch the film to access your engage code.

v1e4-p5fH-gTem-ts6O

Please be aware that this code is case-sensitive and you will need to include the dashes within the passcode, but not when entering the ISBN. For further technical support, please visit www.EN-gage.co.uk

CREDIT MANAGEMENT AND DEBT CONTROL

Qualifications and Credit Framework

Level 4 Diploma in Accounting

British Library Cataloguing-in-Publication Data

A catalogue record for this book is available from the British Library.

Published by
Kaplan Publishing UK
Unit 2, The Business Centre
Molly Millars Lane
Wokingham
Berkshire
RG41 2QZ

ISBN 978-0-85732-375-0

The text in this material and any others made available by any Kaplan Group company does not amount to advice on a particular matter and should not be taken as such. No reliance should be placed on the content as the basis for any investment or other decision or in connection with any advice given to third parties. Please consult your appropriate professional adviser as necessary. Kaplan Publishing Limited and all other Kaplan group companies expressly disclaim all liability to any person in respect of any losses or other claims, whether direct, indirect, incidental, consequential or otherwise arising in relation to the use of such materials.

Printed and bound in Great Britain.

We are grateful to the Association of Accounting Technicians for permission to reproduce past assessment materials and example tasks based on the new syllabus. The solutions to past answers and similar activities in the style of the new syllabus have been prepared by Kaplan Publishing.

CONTENTS

STUDY TEXT AND WORKBOOK

INTRODUCTION

HOW TO USE THESE MATERIALS

These Kaplan Publishing learning materials have been carefully designed to make your learning experience as easy as possible and to give you the best chance of success in your AAT assessments.

They contain a number of features to help you in the study process.

The sections on the Unit Guide, the Assessment and Study Skills should be read before you commence your studies.

They are designed to familiarise you with the nature and content of the assessment and to give you tips on how best to approach your studies.

STUDY TEXT

This study text has been specially prepared for the revised AAT qualification introduced in July 2010.

It is written in a practical and interactive style:

- key terms and concepts are clearly defined

- all topics are illustrated with practical examples with clearly worked solutions based on sample tasks provided by the AAT in the new examining style

- frequent activities throughout the chapters ensure that what you have learnt is regularly reinforced

- 'pitfalls' and 'examination tips' help you avoid commonly made mistakes and help you focus on what is required to perform well in your examination.

- practice activities can be completed at the end of each chapter

WORKBOOK

The workbook comprises:

Practice activities at the end of each chapter with solutions at the end of this text, to reinforce the work covered in each chapter.

The questions are divided into their relevant chapters and students may either attempt these questions as they work through the textbook, or leave some or all of these until they have completed the textbook as a final revision of what they have studied

ICONS

The study chapters include the following icons throughout.

They are designed to assist you in your studies by identifying key definitions and the points at which you can test yourself on the knowledge gained.

 Definition

These sections explain important areas of Knowledge which must be understood and reproduced in an assessment

 Example

The illustrative examples can be used to help develop an understanding of topics before attempting the activity exercises

 Activity

These are exercises which give the opportunity to assess your understanding of all the assessment areas.

KAPLAN PUBLISHING

UNIT GUIDE

Credit management and debt control is divided into two units but for the purposes of assessment these units will be combined.

Principles of Credit Management (Knowledge)

2 credits

Control of Debt and Credit (Skills)

3 credits

Purpose of the units

The AAT has stated that this unit is about understanding the principles of credit and debt management in managing the granting of credit and collection of amounts outstanding from customers in an organisation. The learner will be able to give advice on the grating of credit and also the collection of monies owed in compliance with relevant legislation, good practice and organisational policy. The learner will also be able to give advice on the management of debts and on methods which will minimise the risk to the organisation.

Learning objectives

In the Principles of Credit Management (knowledge) unit:

- Understand how legislation impacts upon credit control
- Understand how to prepare and use information from a variety of sources to manage the organisation's granting of credit
- Be aware of a range of techniques and methods of credit control that may be used within an organisation

In the Control of Debt and Credit (skills) unit:

- Grant credit to customers within organisational guidelines
- Manage the supply of credit

Learning Outcomes and Assessment criteria

The unit consists of five learning outcomes, three for Knowledge and two for Skills, which are further broken down into Assessment criteria. These are set out in the following table with Learning Outcomes in bold type and Assessment criteria listed underneath each Learning Outcome. Reference is also made to the relevant chapter within the text.

Knowledge

To perform this unit effectively you will need to know and understand the following:

		Chapter
1	**Understand how legislation impacts upon credit control**	
1.1	Explain the main features of contract law and remedies for breach of contract in relation to the credit the organisation offers its customers	1
1.2	Define the terms and conditions associated with contracts relating to the granting of credit	1
1.3	Explain the importance of data protection legislation and how it applies to credit management	1
1.4	Explain legal and administrative procedures for the collection of debts	1, 4
1.5	Explain the effect of bankruptcy and insolvency on organisations	1
2	**Understand how to prepare and use information from a variety of sources to manage the organisation's granting of credit**	
2.1	Explain the importance of liquidity management	2, 4
2.2	Identify the information requirements for credit control	2, 3, 4
2.3	Identify sources of credit status and other related information including: Credit rating agencies; supplier references; bank references; analysis of the accounts; colleagues; official publications	2

		Chapter
2.4	Explain methods of analysing credit control information including: age analysis; average periods of credit given and received; incidence of bad and doubtful debts	2, 3
2.5	Identify a range of methods of analysing information on trade receivables	2, 3, 4
3	**Be aware of a range of techniques and methods of credit control that may be used within an organisation**	
3.1	Explain the reasons for offering discounts for prompt payment and identify the effects of offering such a discount	2
3.2	Identify a range of methods for the collection and management of debts and explain the appropriateness of each method	2, 4

Skills

To perform this unit effectively you will need to be able to do the following.

		Chapter
1	**Grant credit to customers within organisational guidelines**	
1.1	Evaluate the current credit status of customers and potential customers	2, 3, 4
1.2	Agree credit terms with customers in accordance with the organisation's policies	2, 4
1.3	Open new accounts for those customers with an established credit status	4
1.4	Agree changes to credit levels or credit terms with customers	3, 4
1.5	Discuss tactfully the reasons for refusing or extending credit with customers	4
2	**Manage the supply of credit**	
2.1	Regularly monitor and analyse information relating to trade receivables' accounts	3, 4

		Chapter
2.2	Promptly send information regarding significant outstanding accounts and potential bad debts to relevant individuals within the organisation	3, 4
2.3	Negotiate with trade receivables in a courteous and profession manner and accurately record the outcome of negotiations	4
2.4	In accordance with organisational procedures select debt recovery methods appropriate to individual outstanding trade receivables	4
2.5	Make recommendations to write off bad debts and make provisions for doubtful debts based upon a realistic analysis of all know factors	2, 4

Delivery guidance

The AAT have provided delivery guidance giving further details of the way in which the unit will be assessed.

Understand how legislation impacts upon credit control.

Candidates will need to demonstrate that they understand how legislation impacts upon the credit control function. Whilst the credit controller does not need to be a qualified lawyer, there is some basic legislation which candidates need to understand and be able to define and explain.

Explain the main features of contract law and remedies for breach of contract in relation to the credit the organisation offers its customers.

In order to ensure that money is received for the sale of goods or the provision of services the credit controller needs to be able to explain the main features of contract law, which include offer and acceptance, remedies available in order to collect outstanding amounts, which include an action for price, and remedies available in the case of customer insolvency, which include retention of title claims.

The legislation that impacts upon credit control includes contract law. Candidates need to have knowledge, understanding, and be able to define and explain the essential characteristics of a contract (including offer, acceptance and consideration).

Candidates need to explain the main documents which form the contract (written order from a customer) and those which are simply an invitation to treat (trade price list).

Other relevant legislation

Trade Descriptions Act – candidates need to understand that it is a criminal offence to make a false statement or to make a misleading statement. Candidates may have to comment on whether a scenario is in breach of this act

Unfair Contract Terms Act – candidates need to understand that unfair terms cannot be part of a contract

Sale of Goods Act 1979 – candidates need to understand when the Sale of Goods Act applies, when title to the goods pass, what conditions can be attached and the key terms of "satisfactory quality", "fit for purpose", "as described"

Consumer Credit Act 1974 – candidates need to understand the key terms of the act.

Late Payment of Commercial Debts (Interest) Act 1998

Candidates may be required to define key terms of the above legislation

Remedies for breach of contract

Candidates need to understand and be able to describe and explain the main remedies for breach of contract including damages and specific performance.

Define the terms and conditions associated with contracts relating to the granting of credit.

Candidates need to be able to define the terms and conditions associated with contracts including offer, acceptance, intention to create legal relations, consideration, capacity to create a contract, consent to the terms, legal and possible, void contracts, voidable contracts and unenforceable contracts.

Explain the importance of data protection legislation and how it applies to credit management.

Candidates need to be able to explain the importance of data protection legislation and how it affects both company and individual customers. Candidates need to understand that the Data Protection Act applies to individuals and not companies. Candidates need to be able to explain how the act applies to credit management for example, the security and use of data.

Explain legal and administrative procedures for the collection of debts.

Candidates need to be able to explain the administrative process for the collection of outstanding accounts. This process starts with the receipt of an order and finishes with the posting of the cash received from the customer. Candidates need to be able to explain the stages in the process and explain the importance of each stage and how earlier stages such as establishing the contract are fundamental to ensuring that customers pay on time or that action can be taken which will result in the successful collection of a debt.

Candidates need to be able to explain the legal and administrative procedures which must be followed for collecting amounts outstanding from customers. These are:

(1) Small claims court action

(2) County court action

(3) High court action

(4) Ways to enforce the judgement – garnishee order, warrant of execution, warrant of delivery, attachment of earnings, charging order

(5) The role of the debt collection agency

(6) The role of solicitors

Explain the effect of bankruptcy and insolvency on organisations.

Candidates need to be able to explain how the bankruptcy or insolvency of a customer may impact on the organisation. Candidates need to understand that supplying goods or services to a customer is an unsecured debt and that in the event of the insolvency of a customer, often little or no money will be received in lieu of the amount outstanding. Candidates need to be able to explain the types of personal insolvency and company insolvency and what action can be taken.

Understand how to prepare and use information from a variety of sources to manage the organisation's granting of credit.

Candidates will need to demonstrate that they understand how to prepare and use information from various sources to manage the granting of credit. The information used to assess credit can be either externally generated or internally generated. The main types of externally generated information are trade credit references, bank references, credit reference agency reports, statutory accounts, management accounts provided by the customer and credit circle meetings. The main types of internally generated information include trading history (for existing customers), information from the sales department, and reports generated from external information such as ratio calculations.

Candidates need to have an understanding of why this information is needed and explain how to use it. Candidates may be required to explain the usefulness of various types of information and explain how to select the most appropriate type to use in a given scenario. This learning outcome may also be assessed indirectly by requiring candidates to apply their understanding to a given scenario and recommend a course of action.

Key to the management of credit is the information available for the assessment of whether to grant credit in the first place. There is often a large range of data available and it is important to know the types of data, how it can be used, and the integrity of the data.

Explain the importance of liquidity management.

Candidates need to be able to explain the importance of liquidity management and how an effective credit control function is fundamental to the liquidity of the business. For most businesses all their turnover is made on credit terms and therefore it is critical to manage the process in order to ensure that sales are only made to organisations which, it has been assessed, will pay to terms and that timely collection of these amounts is taken.

- Candidates need to be able to explain the importance of liquidity management and how an effective credit control function is fundamental to the liquidity of the business.

- Candidates need to be able to explain the difference between a cash sale and a credit sale and the risks associated with a credit sale.

- Candidates need to be able to explain the effect that increasing credit terms has on the cash flow of the business.

- Candidates may be required to explain the cost to the business of extending credit terms or giving cash discounts for prompt payment and its impact on liquidity management.

- Candidates need to be able to describe the main features of invoice discounting and factoring and explain how they can aid the liquidity management of the business. Credit insurance may be required as part of a factoring arrangement or may simply be another tool to aid liquidity management. Candidates may be required to explain the main features of credit insurance, how it aids credit control and its limitations.

Identify the information requirements for credit control.

Candidates need to be able to identify information required for credit control purposes. This information includes both internally generated and externally generated information. Candidates also need to be able to identify those requirements which are specific to a particular type of organisation.

- Candidates need to understand that a company has access to internal and external information and that different types of organisation will need to consider different types of information.

- Candidates need to be able to explain how to select and use various information provided.

- Candidates need to be able to explain the difference between the supply of goods and the supply of services and how the information requirements may be different.

Candidates may be required to explain why it is important to regularly monitor trade receivable accounts, explain what information should be monitored and how that information could be analysed.

Identify sources of credit status and other related information.

Candidates will need to be familiar with the types and structure of credit information. Candidates may be required to explain and describe the most appropriate type of information to be used in a particular case and explain how the information can be used in order to decide whether or not credit should be given. Below is the list of information which candidates need to be able to identify, describe and explain:

- Credit rating agencies reports

- Supplier references

- Bank references

- Statutory accounts filed at companies house

- Management accounts if available

- Information provided by colleagues

- Official publications

Explain methods of analysing credit control information.

Candidates need to be able to explain the following methods of analysing credit control information:

- Age analysis – an explanation of what an age analysis is, the importance of an accurate and timely age analysis, how to use an aged analysis and why it is needed in order to efficiently manage credit

- Average periods of credit given and received – an explanation of what is an average period of credit and how a rapidly expanding turnover can affect the measure of the average period of credit

- Incidence of bad and doubtful debts – an explanation of a bad debt and a doubtful debt and how each affects the cash flow of the organisation

Identify a range of methods of analysing information on trade receivables.

Candidates need to be able to identify a range of methods of analysing information on trade receivables including:

- Aged analysis
- Trading history
- Average periods of credit
- 80/20 rule
- Materiality
- Status reports

Be aware of a range of techniques and methods of credit control that may be used within an organisation.

Candidates will need to be aware of the generic credit control process and the techniques and methods that may be used to efficiently collect outstanding customer accounts. Candidates may be required to explain how to communicate with customers, when to communicate with customers, when to instruct a debt collection agency, when to instruct solicitors and when to issue proceedings.

Candidates need to be aware that there is a range of techniques and methods for the collection of outstanding monies. These include the correct application of contract law, various ways to communicate with the customer and various time frames for this communication. The type of communication will depend on the nature of the goods or services. It is unlikely that a stationery company will meet face to face to discuss payment terms, whereas a defence contractor with a multi-million-pound order is likely to have detailed face-to-face meetings to agree prices and payment schedules, probably with interim payments during the contract.

Explain the reasons for offering discounts for prompt payment and identify the effects of offering such a discount.

Candidates need to explain how offering discounts aids the liquidity of the organisation and explain how discounts can improve cash flow of the organisation. Candidates need also to be able to explain the cost of offering discounts and identify the effects.

Identify a range of methods for the collection and management of debts and explain the appropriateness of each method.

Candidates need to be able to identify methods for the collection and management of debts and explain the appropriateness of each method.

These methods include

- Clear credit control policy

- Written communication (the sending of invoices, statements, solicitors letters)

- The use of telecommunications (contact via the telephone, email, internet)

- Restricting future trade (placing on stop), reducing credit limits, reducing payment terms.

- The use of third parties such as debt collection agencies, factoring companies, credit insurance companies, solicitors

- Small claims summons, County Court summons, High Court summons

- The use of the Late Payment of Commercial Debts (Interest) Act 1998

Grant credit to customers within organisational guidelines.

Successful candidates will be able to grant credit to customers by following good practice, reviewing customer information, considering a range of factors having particular regard to organisational guidelines. Candidates need to be able to select and use a range of tools when granting credit.

Evaluate the current credit status of customers and potential customers.

Candidates will be required to evaluate the current credit status of existing customers and potential customers. This process will be undertaken by using a variety of information collected from both internal and external sources. The information which may be provided for evaluation includes the following:

- Credit rating agencies reports Supplier references

- Bank references

- Statutory accounts filed at companies house

- Management accounts

- Credit circle reports

- Information provided by colleagues

- Official publications.

Candidates will be required to extract relevant information and possibly prepare calculations based upon the information provided. Candidates will be required to prepare ratio calculations based upon published financial information and management accounting information. Candidates may be required to explain and use ratios to evaluate credit status. Candidates may also be required to use a credit scoring system where they have to calculate a credit score based upon a range of performance indicators.

The following financial performance indicators may be assessed:

- Liquidity indicators
    - Current ratio
    - Quick ratio
    - Trade receivable days
    - Trade payable days
    - Stock turnover
    - Working capital cycle
- Profitability indicators
    - Gross profit margin
    - Net profit margin
    - Interest cover
    - Return on capital employed
- Debt indicators
    - Gearing ratio – total debt (short term and long term) / total debt plus equity
    - Short term debt ratio – short term debt as a percentage of total debt
- Cash flow indicators
    - EBITDA – earnings before interest, tax, depreciation and amortisation -EBITDA interest cover
    - EBITDA/interest payable (profit and loss account) or EBITDA/interest paid (cash flow statement, if available)
    - EBITDA to total debt

Agree credit terms with customers in accordance with the organisation's policies.

Once the customer's information has been assessed, credit terms can be agreed. Candidates may be given the organisation's policy and required to set appropriate terms. This may include size of any credit limit and terms of payment of invoices as well as terms such as retention of title. Candidates may be required to decide on the size of a credit limit based upon the expected orders notified by the sales department. For example, a new customer may have passed the evaluation stage and the sales department expects to receive weekly orders of £5,000. Clearly a credit limit of £10,000 will not be sufficient.

Credit insurance may be used and this may inform the decision as to whether to agree credit and set appropriate levels. Candidates need to understand credit insurance and may be required to explain a given credit insurance opinion. Candidates may also be required to advise management on whether to trade with a new customer where credit insurance has been refused.

Open new accounts for those customers with an established credit status.

Candidates may be provided with a credit control policy and procedure for the opening of accounts for new customers. Candidates may be required to explain the policy and procedure and the reasons for the stages or they may be presented with a selection on new customers and required to apply the policy to decide which new customers should be given credit.

Agree changes to credit levels or credit terms with customers.

Candidates may be required to agree changes to current levels of credit in response from a request from a customer or salesman. Examinations may provide additional information and require candidates to assess whether the credit levels or terms should be changed. For example a new customer may be given a £10,000 credit limit and after trading for several months place an order for £15,000. The decision will depend on an assessment to include the trading history of the customer and whether they have kept within their current limit and paid to terms.

Discuss tactfully the reasons for refusing or extending credit with customers

Candidates may be required to draft a response to a customer's request for credit where this request has been refused. Candidates may be required to explain how the refusal of credit should be made and what should be included in a refusal. The refusal should be polite, explain the reasons for refusal, and explain what the company could do to improve their chances of obtaining credit in future including trading on a cash basis to establish a trading history.

Manage the supply of credit.

Candidates need to be able to manage the supply of credit and prepare information to aid the collection of outstanding amounts on a timely basis.

Regularly monitor and analyse information relating to trade receivables' accounts.

Candidates may be required to monitor trade receivable accounts including the preparation of an aged trade receivable report, compliance with payment terms, monitor and implement the organisations policy in respect of placing accounts on hold.

Candidates may be required to analyse an aged trade receivable report and make recommendations as to the action to be taken for individual accounts. Candidates may also be provided with a credit control policy and required to apply this policy to a range of trade receivable accounts stating the action to be taken.

Promptly send information regarding significant outstanding accounts and potential bad debts to relevant individuals within the organisation.

Candidates may be required to prepare an email/ memo in response to a specific request, or as part of the monitoring of trade receivables, regarding significant outstanding amounts and suggest actions to taken and provisions to be made. This could include the suggestion to place an account on hold, instruct a debt collection agency or issue legal proceedings and to make a provision.

Negotiate with trade receivables in a courteous and professional manner and accurately record the outcome of negotiations.

Candidates may be required to prepare a telephone brief or letter which outlines the discussions/ negotiations which have been entered into with a customer. For example, a customer may owe an amount of money and is offering to pay by instalments. It may have been decided by the credit controller that the customer will be allowed to pay over say three or four instalments and that legal proceedings will not be entered into unless the instalments are not paid

In accordance with organisational procedures select debt recovery methods appropriate to individual outstanding trade receivables.

Candidates may be given an aged trade receivable report which requires analysis and recommended actions. Candidates need to be able to consider the aged trade receivable analysis and supplementary information in order to select an appropriate recovery method. Methods include a telephone call, letter or statement, use of a debt collection agency, legal proceedings or possible negotiating with an insolvent company or insolvency practitioner.

Make recommendations to write off bad debts and make provisions for doubtful debts based upon a realistic analysis of all known factors.

Candidates will be required to recommend which outstanding amounts should be written off and provisions that should be made.

KAPLAN PUBLISHING

THE ASSESSMENT

The format of the assessment

The assessment will be divided into two parts and consist of:

Part 1 covers:

- Key credit management concepts

There are 27 objective questions in this section

Part 2 is a mini project that will have 2 tasks:

- The assessment of credit status for the purpose of granting credit

- The assessment of aged trade receivable analysis for the recommendation of actions and provisions

The assessment material will normally be delivered online and assessed locally. Learners will be required to demonstrate competence in all parts of the assessment.

Time allowed

The time allowed for this assessment is **180 minutes.**

STUDY SKILLS

Preparing to study

Devise a study plan

Determine which times of the week you will study.

Split these times into sessions of at least one hour for study of new material. Any shorter periods could be used for revision or practice.

Put the times you plan to study onto a study plan for the weeks from now until the assessment and set yourself targets for each period of study – in your sessions make sure you cover the whole course, activities and the associated questions in the workbook at the back of the manual.

If you are studying more than one unit at a time, try to vary your subjects as this can help to keep you interested and see subjects as part of wider knowledge.

When working through your course, compare your progress with your plan and, if necessary, re-plan your work (perhaps including extra sessions) or, if you are ahead, do some extra revision / practice questions.

Effective studying

Active reading

You are not expected to learn the text by rote, rather, you must understand what you are reading and be able to use it to pass the assessment and develop good practice.

A good technique is to use SQ3Rs – Survey, Question, Read, Recall, Review:

1 **Survey the chapter**

   Look at the headings and read the introduction, knowledge, skills and content, so as to get an overview of what the chapter deals with.

2 **Question**

   Whilst undertaking the survey ask yourself the questions you hope the chapter will answer for you.

3 Read

Read through the chapter thoroughly working through the activities and, at the end, making sure that you can meet the learning objectives highlighted on the first page.

4 Recall

At the end of each section and at the end of the chapter, try to recall the main ideas of the section / chapter without referring to the text. This is best done after short break of a couple of minutes after the reading stage.

5 Review

Check that your recall notes are correct.

You may also find it helpful to re-read the chapter to try and see the topic(s) it deals with as a whole.

Note taking

Taking notes is a useful way of learning, but do not simply copy out the text.

The notes must:

- be in your own words
- be concise
- cover the key points
- well organised
- be modified as you study further chapters in this text or in related ones.

Trying to summarise a chapter without referring to the text can be a useful way of determining which areas you know and which you don't.

Three ways of taking notes

1 Summarise the key points of a chapter

2 Make linear notes

A list of headings, subdivided with sub-headings listing the key points.

If you use linear notes, you can use different colours to highlight key points and keep topic areas together.

Use plenty of space to make your notes easy to use.

3 Try a diagrammatic form

The most common of which is a mind map.

To make a mind map, put the main heading in the centre of the paper and put a circle around it.]

Draw lines radiating from this to the main sub-headings which again have circles around them.

Continue the process from the sub-headings to sub-sub-headings.

Highlighting and underlining

You may find it useful to underline or highlight key points in your study text – but do be selective.

You may also wish to make notes in the margins.

Revision phase

Kaplan has produced material specifically designed for your final examination preparation for this unit.

These include pocket revision notes and a bank of revision questions specifically in the style of the new syllabus.

Further guidance on how to approach the final stage of your studies is given in these materials.

Further reading

In addition to this text, you should also read the "Student section" of the "Accounting Technician" magazine every month to keep abreast of any guidance from the examiners.

TERMINOLOGY FOR CRMC

There are different terms used to mean the same thing – you will need to be aware of both sets of terminology.

UK GAAP	IAS
Final accounts	Financial statements
Trading and profit and loss account	Income statement
Turnover or Sales	Revenue or Sales revenue
Balance sheet	Statement of financial position
Fixed assets	Non-current Assets
Net book value	Carrying amount
Tangible assets	Property, plant and equipment
Stock	Inventory
Trade Debtors	Trade Receivables
Trade Creditors	Trade Payables
Long term liabilities	Non-current liabilities
Capital	Equity
Profit and loss balance	Retained earnings
Net Profit	Profit for the year

Legislation

1

Introduction

In this chapter we start by looking at some of the legislation that affects granting credit to customers.

KNOWLEDGE

Explain the main features of contract law and remedies for breach of contract in relation to the credit the organisation offers its customer (1.1)

Define the terms and conditions associated with contracts relating to the granting of credit (1.2)

Explain the importance of data protection legislation and how it applies to credit management (1.3)

Explain legal and administrative procedures for the collection of debts (1.4)

Explain the effect of bankruptcy and insolvency on organisations (1.5)

CONTENTS

1 Contract law

1.1 Introduction

Control of the credit given to a customer is important for any company. Most companies therefore appoint a **credit controller** whose responsibility is to give appropriate credit terms to customers and ensure these terms are kept. **Debtors** are an important part of **working capital** and **careful management** of this asset is required to maintain the company's **liquidity**.

First of all it is important to understand the legal background to contracts and credit arrangements.

1.2 Nature of a contract

The sale of goods and services is a type of contract and therefore the credit controller must ensure that each party abides by this contract.

 Definition

A contract is a legally binding agreement between two parties.

The **law of contract** is the branch of the civil law which determines whether or not a promise is legally binding (i.e. enforceable by a court of law).

1.3 The essential characteristics of a contract

There are **seven** fundamental requirements if a contract is to be valid:

- **offer** and **acceptance** (i.e. an agreement);

- the **intention to create legal relations** (i.e. the parties must be willing to submit to the authority of the law and be bound by their contracts);

- **consideration**, in that both parties must do, or promise to do, something as their side of the contract;

- **written formalities** must be observed in some situations;

- the parties must have the **capacity**, or ability, **to contract and submit** themselves to the authority of the law (children and mentally disordered people are restricted);

- the parties must genuinely **consent to the terms** of the contract in that they must not have been mistaken by the contract terms, or lied to in negotiations – there must be **certainty of terms**
- the contract itself must be both **legal** and **possible**.

The key factors are a basic understanding of offer, acceptance and consideration which will be considered below.

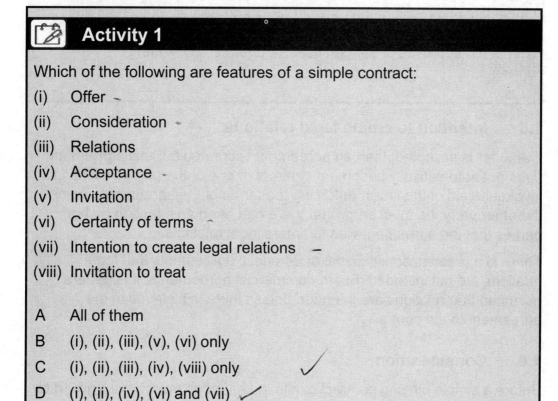

Activity 1

Which of the following are features of a simple contract:

(i)   Offer

(ii)   Consideration

(iii)   Relations

(iv)   Acceptance

(v)   Invitation

(vi)   Certainty of terms

(vii) Intention to create legal relations

(viii) Invitation to treat

A   All of them

B   (i), (ii), (iii), (v), (vi) only

C   (i), (ii), (iii), (iv), (viii) only

D   (i), (ii), (iv), (vi) and (vii)

1.4   Offer and acceptance

An **offer** may be addressed to a specific person, to a group of people or to the world at large. However, acceptance of the offer must be made specifically.

It is important to distinguish between an **offer** – which can be accepted by a mere **act, express or implied of the other party**, after which the contract is complete – and **an invitation to treat** where the resulting **action of the other party is the offer**. Advertisements, price tickets in shops etc are an invitation to treat. They are an invitation to the potential customer to make an offer.

Acceptance is the **final expression** of assent to the terms of the offer. To be effective, the acceptance must be made while the offer is still in force; it must be **absolute**, **unqualified** and **communicated** to the offeror by word or action.

Offer and acceptance constitute agreement.

Example

Joseph offers to sell his car to Benjamin. Benjamin accepts so long as the car has a valid MOT certificate. This does not constitute an agreement as Benjamin's response has a criterion that must be met. Once Joseph proves he has a valid MOT and Benjamin accepts this certificate then there has been an offer (to sell the car) and acceptance (Benjamin approves of the certificate) therefore constituting an agreement.

1.5   Intention to create legal relations

If an offer is accepted, then an agreement is created but this agreement does not automatically become a contract. If one of the parties wishes to invoke the aid of the law in enforcing the terms of the agreement against the other party, he must show that there had been an intention by both parties that the agreement was to create legal relations.

There is a presumption in social or domestic agreements that legal relations are not intended. But in commercial agreements, it is generally assumed that relations are intended unless there is a clause in the agreement to the contrary.

1.6   Consideration

Before a simple binding contract exists, both parties must have **agreed to provide something of value to the other**. The price which each has to pay is termed the consideration and converts the mere promises of the parties into bargains enforceable by the courts.

Definition

Consideration can be defined as 'some right, interest, profit or benefit accruing to one party, or some forbearance, detriment, loss or responsibility given, suffered or undertaken by the other'.

Example

Joseph offers to sell his car to Benjamin for £2,500. Benjamin agrees to pay £2,500 for Joseph's car. There has been offer and acceptance and consideration – a simple contract has been formed.

 Activity 2

Raphael has a notice in his shop window saying that the books he has for sale are half price. This is an example of:

A   Offer

B   Acceptance

C   Invitation to treat ✓

D   Consideration

 Activity 3

Barry is ordering an Indian takeaway on the telephone and says he will pay when he picks up the order. Which of the following would constitute consideration?

A   Placing the order

B   Paying for the order ✓

C   Saying he will pay for the order

D   Picking up the order

1.7   Void, voidable and unenforceable contracts

A **void** contract is one that **cannot be enforced by law**. An agreement to carry out an illegal act or an agreement that is impossible to carry out are examples of void contracts.

A **voidable** contract is a valid contract that **can be nullified** – one party is bound to a contract but the other party is not so can withdraw from the contract. If this happens then the contract becomes void. A contract between an adult and a minor is an example of a voidable contract as the adult is bound by the contract but the minor is not as they are not of legal age.

An **unenforceable contract** is one that is **valid** (i.e. meets all the requirements listed above) but **if one party withdraws** from the contract the **courts of law will not enforce** them to meet the requirements of the contract.

 Activity 4

A void contract is a contract that:

A   Is valid

B   Can be enforced by the law

C   Can be nullified

D   Cannot be enforced by the law ✔

---

2 Other legislation

2.1   Trade Descriptions Act

The Trade Descriptions Act states that manufacturers, retailer and the service industry must **correctly describe what they are selling**. The goods or service must be as described, of satisfactory quality and be fit for purpose. It is a **criminal offence to make a false or misleading statement** about the goods or services being provided i.e. **misrepresented** in any way.

2.2   Unfair Contract Terms Act

Contracts must be written in **language that is understandable** and any part of the contract that acts more favourably for the vendor than the consumer is unfair and not binding.

This is the most important statute affecting exclusion clauses and is largely restricted to business liability i.e. liability arising during business or from occupation of premises for business purposes. It is not possible to exclude liability for death or personal injury and all other losses are subject to a test of reasonableness.

2.3   Sale of Goods Act 1979

The sale of goods act states that as a buyer you have 3 statutory rights:

1   The seller has the right to be selling the goods/providing the service

2   That the goods match the description provided by the seller i.e. the goods are 'as described' and 'fit for purpose'

3   The goods are of 'satisfactory quality'

The sale of goods act **applied when the title of the goods has passed from the vendor to the buyer.**

2.4 Consumer Credit Act 1974

The Consumer Credit Act 1974 requires:

- Businesses that offer goods or services on credit or lend money to consumers to be licensed by the Office of Fair Trading. Trading without a licensing arrangement is a criminal offence and can result in a fine and/or imprisonment.

- That the borrower can settle a regulated consumer credit agreement early by giving notice to the lender and paying the amount due less a rebate. The borrower is also entitled to information about the amount needed to settle.

- The seller lays down rules requiring information to be given to borrowers or hirers before entry into a consumer credit or hire agreement.

2.5 Late Payment of Commercial Debts (Interest) Act 1998

The late payment act allows businesses to charge other business customers interest on overdue amounts. Interest can be charged:

- 30 days after the goods are supplied or the service is completed,

- 30 days after receipt of invoice (or the customer is told the amount due is payable).

- The agreed date for payment.

The "statutory interest" rate chargeable is the Bank of England base rate plus 8%. This is to allow small business to cover late payments by bank borrowings.

Activity 5

Calvin is sold some lime cordial by Hobbs but when Calvin opens the bottle it is actually lemonade. Calvin can claim for breach of contract due to:

A   Fiduciary misconduct

B   Misrepresentation ✓   ✓

C   Misuse of Sales Act

D   Unfair Contract Terms Act

3 Data Protection Act

3.1 Introduction

Due to the growth in the use of computer technology the Data Protection Act 1998 was introduced to make **certain restrictions** on the use of data about **individuals** and the **use of personal data**. It is likely that your organisation will hold computer data about credit customers and therefore you need to be aware of the broad outlines of the Act. However it is important to realise that the Act relates to data **held about individuals not about organisations** so will only be relevant to non-corporate customers or to data about individuals who belong to a customer organisation.

3.2 Definitions

Personal data is information held about an individual, not only factual information but also expressions of opinion about that individual.

Data users are individuals or organisations who use personal data.

A computer bureau is an individual or organisation which processes personal data for data users or allows data users to process personal data on its equipment.

3.3 The Key Principles of the Act

- Data may only be used for the **specific purposes** for which it was collected.

- Data **must not be disclosed** to other parties without the consent of the individual whom it is about, unless there is legislation or other overriding legitimate reason to share the information (for example, the prevention or detection of crime). It is an offence for Other Parties to obtain this personal data without authorisation.

- **Individuals have a right of access to the information held about them,** subject to certain exceptions (for example, information held for the prevention or detection of crime).

- Personal information may be **kept for no longer than is necessary** and must be kept up to date.

- Personal information **may not be sent outside the European Economic Area** unless the individual whom it is about has consented or adequate protection is in place, for example by the use of a prescribed form of contract to govern the transmission of the data.

- Subject to some exceptions for organisations that only do very simple processing, and for domestic use, all entities that process personal information must **register with the Information Commissioner's Office**.

- Entities holding personal information are required to have adequate **security measures in place**. Those include technical measures (such as firewalls) and organisational measures (such as staff training).

- Subjects have the right to have **factually incorrect information corrected** (note: this does not extend to matters of opinion)

- All data users and computer bureaux have to **register with the Data Protection Registrar** – the data user must then only hold data and use data for the purposes which are registered.

- Processing of personal data is forbidden except in the following circumstances:

    - with the consent of the individual

    - due to a legal obligation

    - due to a contractual obligation

    - due to a contractual arrangement

    - in the public interest

    - to protect the vital interests of the individual.

- If data is obtained from a third party the data subject must be given:

    - the identity of the controller of the data

    - the purposes for which the data is being processed

    - the data that will be disclosed and to whom.

- Data subjects have the right to a copy of the data held, the right to know why the data is being processed and the logic behind the processing. Data subjects may seek compensation through the courts for damage or distress caused by the loss, destruction, inaccuracy or unauthorised disclosure of personal data.

- Data subjects can apply to the courts or Registrar for inaccurate data to be corrected or removed from the data user's files.

Activity 6

The Data Protection Act applies to (pick as many as appropriate):

A   Data about individuals, companies and government departments

B   Data about individuals only ✓

C   Data about companies only

D   Data about companies and individuals only

E   Only manual records

F   Only computer records

G   All records held by the company ✓

H   Only records of opinions

4 Legal action

4.1 Introduction

Legal action can be taken to force an overdue debtor to pay its debts. Before commencing, it is wise to ensure that:

(a) the debt is not disputed

(b) the name and trading style of the debtor is accurate i.e. sole trader, partnership or company, and

(c) the customer has sufficient assets to pay the bill.

4.2 Remedies for breach of contract

This section examines the legal remedies that may be available to any injured party as a result of the breach of a contract. We shall be paying particular attention to the remedies that are of use to an unpaid creditor/supplier to collect amounts that are due to them.

In such a situation, the injured party may have one or more of the following remedies:

(a) He may recover **damages** for any loss suffered as a result of the breach by bringing an **action for damages** for breach of contract.

(b) If the breach consists of the other party's failure to pay a debt (i.e. the contractually agreed price or other remuneration due under the contract), the appropriate course for the injured party is to bring an action for the **agreed sum** to recover that amount, this is an **action for price.**

(c) He may get a court injunction to force the other party to **complete the contract** – this is usually only done if the action for damages is not sufficient. This is known as an action for **specific performance**.

(d) The seller of the goods may put in the contract that the **'goods remain the property of the seller until payment has been received'**. This means that the seller has **retention of title** and if there is non-payment can **retain the ownership** of the goods.

4.3 How to bring a dispute to court

If threats of legal action are carried out for a debtor who has not paid then the initial step is to instruct a solicitor. The solicitor will require details of the goods or services provided, the date the liability arose, the exact name and trading status of the debtor, any background information such as disputes in the past and a copy of any invoices that are unpaid.

In some cases after the solicitor has got involved there may be a negotiated settlement between the creditor and debtor as the debtor does not want to run the risk of going to court. However in other situations the case will be taken to court.

4.4 Appropriate courts

If the claim is for less than £5,000 then the claim will be made using the Small Claims Track of the County Court.

Any claims for more than £5,000 will normally be dealt with in the County Court.

Claims higher than £15,000 can be heard in the High Court.

4.5 Procedure

The appropriate court, once it has received all of the paperwork will issue a summons to the debtor requiring an acknowledgement of service of the summons. If the debtor does not reply then the judgement will go against him. The debtor may admit the claim and perhaps offer to pay by instalments. If the creditor does not accept this then the court will determine a suitable method of paying off the debt.

Once the court order has been made then the money must be collected and there are a number of methods of achieving this.

Activity 7

If an outstanding debt is more than £5,000 the court that would deal with any action would be:

A   The high court

B   An industrial tribunal

C   A small claims court

D   The county court ✓

4.6   The seizure of goods

Seizing goods is effective against businesses with valuable items in their offices, such as computers. The court bailiff is given a '**warrant of execution'**. He will seize the goods and sell them by public auction with the proceeds paid to the creditor.

4.7   Attachment of earnings order

An attachment of earnings order ensures that the **creditor is paid directly by the debtor's employer out of his/her pay packet.**

This is only available against individual debtors who are in employment and is usually very unsuccessful as the court needs to determine the 'protected' earnings of the individual and the debtor's employer needs to co-operate fully. Such a person is likely to change employment frequently which creates further complications in tracing them and taking out fresh attachment orders.

4.8   Garnishee order

A garnishee order allows the **creditor to be paid directly by a debtor of the offending company** i.e., a third party who also owes the defaulting company money.

4.9   Administrative order

Where a debtor has a number of debts totalling less than £5,000 then the **debtor might make regular payments into court** and the **court distributes them** to the creditors on a pro rata basis.

4.10   Charging order

The court can order a charge on the debtor's property and if the **debt is not paid within six months** the **creditor has the right to have the property sold.**

KAPLAN PUBLISHING

4.11 Bankruptcy notice (against a partner or individual)

A bankruptcy notice is usually very effective as few people like to go out of business. For a bankruptcy order to succeed the debt must be in excess of £750, it must be unsecured and the debtor must be domiciled in the UK.

 Activity 8

The normal remedy for breach of contract due to non payment of the debt is:

A   Action for remedy

B   Action for the goods

C   Action for specific performance

D   Action for price ✓

 Activity 9

Retention of title is:

A   The right of the seller to retain ownership of the goods until payment is made ✓

B   The right of the purchaser to retain ownership of the goods received

C   The right of the purchaser to expect that title is retained by the seller even when payment has been received

D   The right of the seller to retain ownership of the goods until a cheque has been posted

 Activity 10

If payment of a debt is not forthcoming what action 'allows the creditor to be paid directly by a debtor of the offending company'

A   Attachment of earning order

B   Garnishee order ✓

C   Administrative order

D   Charging order

5   Bankruptcy and liquidation

5.1   Introduction

Supplying goods or services to a customer is an unsecured debt and if the customer becomes bankrupt or goes into liquidation then often little or no money will be received.

However, if the business is on the verge of bankruptcy and a bankruptcy order is issued, then the official receiver will distribute the assets in the following order:

(a)   secured creditors

(b)   bankruptcy costs

(c)   preferential creditors

(d)   unsecured creditors

(e)   deferred creditors

(f)   the bankrupt.

As an unsecured creditor, the supplier is a long way down the list of payments and even in a bankruptcy may not receive the money owed.

5.2   Consequences of a petition for bankruptcy

The consequences of a petition for bankruptcy against a debtor are:

- if the debtor pays money to any other creditors or disposes of any property then these transactions are void

- any other legal proceedings relating to the debtor's property or debts are suspended

- an interim receiver is appointed to protect the estate.

5.3   Consequences of a bankruptcy order

The consequences of a bankruptcy order are:

- the official receiver takes control of the assets of the business

- a statement of the assets and liabilities is drawn up – this is known as a statement of affairs

- the receiver summons a meeting of creditors within 12 weeks of the bankruptcy order

- the creditors appoint a trustee in bankruptcy

- the assets of the business are realised and distribution is made to the various creditors in the order given above.

5.4 Liquidation (or winding-up) of a company

A company cannot be dissolved until it is removed from the register of companies, which requires the correct legal procedures to be completed. This means that its assets must be realised (converted into cash) and then applied in payment of its debts (in due order) and any surplus distributed among its members according to their entitlement.

The process commences with a court order or by the members passing a resolution to wind the company up. If a creditor for more than £750 serves a statutory demand for payment at the registered office of the company and the company neglects for three weeks to pay the debt or to secure or compound it to the creditor's reasonable satisfaction, then the company is deemed unable to pay its debts.

5.5 Steps in a liquidation

The following steps will then be taken:

(a) ascertaining that the company is unable to pay its debts

(b) petition for winding up

(c) winding-up order

(d) meeting of creditors

(e) statement of affairs

(f) appointment of liquidator

(g) administration of the company's estate

(h) payment of creditors

5.6 Payment in a liquidation

The order of pay-off of the company's debts is as follows:

(a)   secured creditors, excluding holders of floating charges

(b)   liquidation costs

(c)   preferential creditors

(d)   holders of floating charges

(e)   unsecured creditors

(f)   shareholders.

 Activity 11

What is the correct order of distribution of assets if a bankruptcy order is issued:

A   preferential creditors   *3*

B   deferred creditors   *4*

C   secured creditors _   *1*

D   unsecured creditors   *5*

E   the bankrupt   *6*

F   bankruptcy costs   *2*

---

6   Summary

The sale of goods on credit to a customer is a contract and therefore you need to be aware of the legal background in terms of the general nature of contract law. You must also be aware of the basic provisions of the Data Protection Act and other legal terms and conditions in relation to a contract.

KAPLAN PUBLISHING

Answers to chapter activities

Activity 1

Answer D

Activity 2

Answer C

Activity 3

Answer C

Activity 4

Answer D

Activity 5

Answer B

Activity 6

Answers B and G

Activity 7

Answer D

 Activity 8

Answer D

 Activity 9

Answer A

 Activity 10

Answer B

 Activity 11

Answer C, F, A, D, B, E

KAPLAN PUBLISHING

7 Test your knowledge

Workbook Activity 12

Steph has asked Callum for a price to paint her bedroom. Callum has said he can do it for £300 and Steph has agreed. Nearing the end of the job Callum asks Steph for £50 more as he has underestimated the work. Does Steph have to pay Callum the extra £50?

Yes / No ? ✓

Workbook Activity 13

If payment of a debt is not forthcoming what action allows the creditor to be paid directly by the debtor's employer out of his/her pay packet:

A   Attachment of earning order

B   Garnishee order

C   Administrative order ✓

D   Charging order

Workbook Activity 14

What is the correct order of distribution of assets if a liquidation order is issued:

G   preferential creditors   3

H   shareholders   6

I   secured creditors   1

J   unsecured creditors   4

K   holders of floating charges   5

L   liquidation costs   2

Granting credit

2

Introduction

In this chapter we look at why a business grants credit, the cost of granting credit and what information is required to decide whether to grant credit or extend credit terms and conditions

KNOWLEDGE	CONTENTS
Explain the importance of liquidity management (2.1)	1 The importance of trade receivables
Identity the information requirements for credit control (2.2)	2 Cost of offering credit
Identify sources of credit status and other related information including: credit rating agencies; supplier references; bank references; analysis of the accounts; colleagues; official publications (2.3)	3 Granting credit 4 Credit terms and conditions 5 External sources of information 6 Internal sources of information
Explain methods of analysing credit control information including: Credit rating agencies; supplier references; bank references; analysis of accounts; colleagues; official publications (2.4)	
Identify a range of methods of analysing information on trade receivables (2.5)	
Explain the reason for offering discounts for prompt payment and identify the effects of offering such a discount (3.1)	
Identify a range of methods for the collection and management of debts and explain the appropriateness of each method (3.2)	

SKILLS

Evaluate the current credit status of customers and potential customer (1.1)

Agree credit terms with customers in accordance with the organisation's policies (1.2)

Make recommendations to write off bad debts and make provisions for doubtful debts based upon a realistic analysis of all know factors (2.5)

1 The importance of trade receivables

1.1 Introduction

Payment for goods can either be made by cash or credit. Payment by **cash** (including cheque, credit/debit cards) means that the business received what it is owed for the goods or services at the time they are provided. Payment on **credit** (issue an invoice and payment is received at a later date) means that the business provides the goods or service and payment is received later. This creates trade receivables for the business.

1.2 The trade receivable balancing act

Trade receivables are people who owe you money, the almost inevitable consequence of trading. Trade receivables form part of the **working capital cycle** and as such management of trade receivables is very important in **maintaining the liquidity** of the company.

For many businesses their entire turnover is made on credit terms with very few business-to-business transactions being made for cash and likewise fewer business-to-customer transactions are cash.

Trade receivable management principles involve a series of balancing acts. The following diagram should be remembered.

Balancing costs and benefits of trade receivables

Benefit of granting trade credit	Costs of granting trade credit
	Finance costs
Marketing benefits	Bad debts costs (default)
	Administration costs

The main benefit to the company is that **customers like to be given trade credit**, rather than paying on delivery of goods. Thus, generous credit terms often have a beneficial impact on sales.

Activity 1

Why is liquidity important?

A   to ensure that a company does not make a loss

B   so that the shareholders can see how much return they will get on their investment

C   so that the company can estimate how much cash is tied up in stock and fixed assets

D ✓ so that the company can ensure that cash is available to discharge commitments

2 Cost of offering credit

2.1   Finance cost

The main cost to the company of granting trade credit is the **finance cost**. Trade receivables on the balance sheet do not earn a return i.e. the cash is not in the company's bank account therefore it is not earning interest. This may lead to the company needing to raise extra finance to be able to pay bills e.g. use of an overdraft. A company that demands cash on delivery will have the cash available to pay bills so should not need to use an overdraft in the same manner. A company giving trade credit is effectively financing its trade receivable balances all year round in a similar manner to stock balances.

Example

Z buys an item for £20 on 1 January 20X6 and pays the company one year later on 31 December 20X6.

The company earns a profit of £4 on each unit sold (sales price is £20)

The company has an overdraft, paying interest at 10%.

What profit does the company make from the sale of the unit after allowing for the cost of credit?

Solution

	£
Net profit on sale of one unit	4
Less: Interest on overdraft	(2)
(£20 outstanding receipt × 10%)	
Real profit after credit period costs	2

So the granting of one year's credit has reduced the company's profit margin by 50% which is a substantial cost to the company. A year's credit is probably longer than most companies would grant but even a two month credit period costs a company a substantial percentage of the profit margin, i.e.:

	£
Net profit on sales	4.00
Less: Interest on overdraft	
(using simple interest) £20 × 10% × (2/12)	(0.33)
Real profit after credit period costs	3.67

i.e. (33p/400p) × 100% = 8.25% of the profit is lost.

In other words, it costs the company 8.25% to offer two months' credit to its customers.

If interest rates increase, then the cost of credit will also increase. The main board of directors needs to consider these facts when agreeing credit terms with the credit manager.

2.2 Non-payment of debts

A company granting trade credit may suffer **bad debts** as customers go into liquidation before paying what is due. This cannot happen to a company giving no credit as cash is required on delivery.

Definition

A bad debt is a debt which the credit manager is fairly certain will never be received from the customer.

A bad debt will have an **effect on the cash flow**, as this represents **income which is no longer realisable**. For example suppose that a trade receivable company has gone into liquidation and the final dividend (say 40p in the £) has been paid to creditors, the balancing 60% of the debt has to be written off. This occurs both in the accounts and in the cash flow. The latter will need to be adjusted and, if the debt is large, the credit manager will need to consider the effect on the overall cash balance and take the necessary adjusting steps.

Specific provision for doubtful debts

 Definition

A specific provision for doubtful debts is a provision against a particular debt owed as there is concern than it may not be paid in full.

General provision

 Definition

A general provision is a further provision against normally a percentage of remaining debts which reflects the fact that some debts may not be paid in full

The specific and general provisions together form the doubtful debt provision which is credited in the balance sheet against trade receivables. This provision is an accounting entry only and **does not represent any movement in the cash position.**

2.3 Administrative costs

If a company gives no credit its sales system will often be very simple to operate, and hence cheap. A business giving credit, by contrast, has more expensive recording and collection systems, hence much **higher administrative expenses.**

2.4 Cash or settlement discounts

With some credit agreements there will be a **discount offered** as an **incentive** to pay the money owed within a **certain time frame.** For example, the normal credit period may be 90 days, but the company may be prepared to offer, say, 1% discount for payment within 45 days. This would be described as '1/45, net 90'.

The costs and benefits of a cash discount scheme are summarised below:

Benefits	Costs
Reduction in finance charges	Cost of discount (reduced revenue received)
Reduction in bad debts due to reduced collection period	Extra administrative costs
Improved customer relations and potential extra sales	Potential abuse of scheme (customer takes discount but does not pay early)
Improves short term liquidity as cash received sooner	

2.5 Assessing a proposed discount policy

It is possible to approximate the simple annual cost of offering a discount to trade receivables by using a formula:

$$\frac{d}{100 - d} \times \frac{365}{N - D}$$

where   d   =   discount percentage given

           N   =   normal payment term

           D   =   discount payment term

💡 Example

Current credit terms are payment within 60 days but the anticipated cash flows from these invoiced sales will be:

- 40% in the month the invoice is issued

- 50% in the month after the invoice is issued

- 10% in two months after the invoice is issued.

The finance director is considering introducing a settlement discount of 3% for payments received in the month that the sales invoice is raised. This policy is expected to result in 80% of customers paying within the month of the invoice and the remainder paying in the following month.

Using the above information we can calculate the approximate annual cost of the proposed discount.

The discount was 3% for payment within 30 days whereas the normal credit terms were 60 days.

Annual cost $= \dfrac{d}{100 - d} \times \dfrac{365}{N - D}$

$= \dfrac{3}{100 - 3} \times \dfrac{365}{60 - 30}$

$= 38\%$

As it would cost 38% per annum to offer this discount, it would most certainly be cheaper to borrow from the bank to raise any funds required.

Activity 2

What is the cost of giving a 5% prompt payment discount to customers who pay within 30 days rather than the usual 90 days?

A   21%

B   64%

C   32%

D   3.1%

$\dfrac{5}{95} \times \dfrac{365}{60} = 32\%$

Activity 3

A company is concerned about the size of its trade receivables and its cash flows. It therefore decides to offer a 'prompt payment discount' of 1.5% for payment within 14 days. Without the discount, customers take 60 days' credit.

What is the amount the customer would pay on an invoice of £350 and what is the simple annual interest rate of the discount?

A   £344.75 and 12.1%

B   £297.50 and 39.1%

C   £344.75 and 0.2%

D   £297.50 and 39.7%

$350 \times 98.5\% = 344.75$

$\dfrac{1.5}{98.5} \times \dfrac{365}{46} = 12.1\%$

3 Granting credit

3.1 Introduction

Giving a customer credit terms for payment is always a risk and all companies try to reduce this risk and potential bad debt problems.

There are various ways of obtaining information about customers both from one's own experience and from external sources and references. All available information needs to be collected and assimilated so that appropriate credit terms can be given to the customer. Once agreed, these terms will then form the basis of the contract of sale between the two parties and trading can proceed smoothly.

One of the first steps is to appoint a credit manager or a senior person to take responsibility for the granting of credit terms.

3.2 The credit manager

The purpose of the credit manager in a company is to **protect the company's investment in trade receivables**. This entails ensuring appropriate credit terms are negotiated with customers and are then adhered to. The manager usually reports to the finance director or financial controller; sometimes, however, he may be found within the sales/marketing area. Wherever the manager is placed, it is important that he is **aware of the sales and marketing opportunities and constraints**, as well as confident that the cash flow of the business is not disrupted by inappropriate financial terms.

3.3 Company policy

The credit manager needs to ascertain the basis of the **company's credit terms** (more details below). This may have been decided upon by the finance director, be documented and so merely require implementing. However, most companies are not so well organised and a pattern of credit terms has to be developed by the credit controller in consultation with his superior and the sales department. This has the advantage of allowing a flexible method to develop which can cater for differing situations. But in a large organisation this can lead to uncertainty and areas of doubt and it may be sensible to establish written guidelines and terms of reference. In order to do this, it is necessary to establish two key points – the nature of the market and the authority of the credit manager.

3.4 Nature of the market

Consideration needs to be given to any **seasonal fluctuations**, the expected level of sales, the marketing strategy and the policies of competitors. It is easy to set standards but, if this results in the loss of trade and goodwill, the company will not flourish. So the credit manager must try to keep trade receivables low without losing business.

3.5 Authority of the credit manager

It must be clear who **establishes the credit terms**: the sales manager or the credit manager, or both in consultation – in which case, their joint policy must be clearly documented to avoid any misunderstandings. Also, the credit manager needs to establish whether he has the authority to accept or reject new customers or new orders. The business will be handicapped if there is constant resentment or a feeling of interference by the credit and sales departments, in each other's work and authority. Ideally, this will not arise if good communications are present and each department liaises with the other.

3.7 Evaluating a customer's credit status

The correct evaluation of credit risk is the most **difficult** and the most vital part of the credit manager's role. Regrettably, the credit manager is sometimes merely regarded as a 'credit controller' and the evaluation of the credit risk is left to the sales department, so ignoring the potential contribution to profits which a trained credit manager can make.

It may be tempting to **select safe customers** who will pay promptly, but this will restrict the company's market share and hence its profit share. In order to maximise profits, it is **necessary to sell to 'risky' customers** and it is the process of **evaluating this risk** that is now considered.

It is not only new accounts that need to be considered, the credit manager needs constantly to **review his established customer base** to ensure that they continue to be a safe risk and have not slipped with their payments. Where danger signals are spotted, prompt action is required in consultation with the sales department to decide on future strategy as to whether to continue with sales, restrict sales or even cease trading with the customer.

Remember that if one is dealing with a major customer there are many points to consider and one needs to balance the risk of non-payment against other factors such as the stoppage of production and the laying off of workers.

KAPLAN PUBLISHING

3.8 Sources of information

There are many sources of information from which an assessment can be made regarding the risk of non-payment by a trade receivable. These can be split into two types:

(a) **external sources** – from outside publications, statistics and institutions

(b) **internal sources** – derived from the company's own database, analysis of accounts and direct contacts with the customer.

4 Credit terms and conditions

4.1 Introduction

As sales agreements are contracts, the credit terms are part of this contract. Credit terms have to be drawn up for a company and must take into account the need to maintain both the company's cash flow and a sensible profit margin on the goods sold.

These terms must be **clearly understood** by the customer and it is sensible to print these clearly on the invoice to the customer. The company must be prepared to enforce the terms if the customer is late paying the debt.

Definition

- **Credit limit** – the maximum amount a customer may have outstanding (more detail later in the chapter)

- **Credit term** – the length of time they are allowed to have outstanding amounts.

4.2 Types of credit terms

The most common types of credit term agreed between customer and supplier in the UK are as follows:

(a) **Cash with order** – This is effectively giving no credit, as no work on the order will happen until payment is received.

(b) **Cash before shipment** –This requires payment to be made before delivery and, while it safeguards cash receipts, if the customer refuses the goods at the last minute, a supplier could be left with bespoke articles which cannot easily be sold.

Cash on delivery is much the same in principle but depends on a trustworthy driver to collect the payment and the customer to pay with a bona fide cheque.

(c) **Load over load** is an agreement to pay for the last load before the next delivery is made.

(d) **Net monthly** requires payment of one month's deliveries to be made by the end of the following month. It is not always possible to post invoices exactly to the correct month and so month-end deliveries may not be paid for two months!

Net 30 days means payment 30 days after delivery and so brings forward the payment date on average 15 days earlier than a 'net monthly' agreement.

Net 14 days brings forward payment to 14 days after delivery while **Net 60 days/Net 90** days may be given if the market demands.

(e) **Stage-payments** allow for instalments of the expected total bill to be paid at agreed intervals. It is usual in certain trades (e.g. building and shipping) to make progress payments based on certified work during the course of the contract. Care needs to be taken when negotiating these terms and income matched with expenditure on the project; it is foolish to agree a down payment of 30% and the balance on completion if all the materials – constituting 70% of the final price – have to be paid for before the completion of the contract.

Whether the terms are agreed on a time basis as in (d) and (e) or on a delivery basis as in (a), (b) and (c), the terms must be clearly stated on the invoice and the accounting records must be able to identify customers who are late paying their debts.

4.3 A typical credit control policy and procedure

Credit terms and conditions should be laid out in a document which should be available to new and current trade receivables to review.

A typical credit control policy could be as follows:

New Accounts

- One bank reference and two trade references are required.

- A credit reference agency report and the last three years published accounts for limited companies need to be analysed.

- A credit reference agency report and the last three years accounts for a sole trader need to be analysed.

Existing customers

- A credit reference agency report to be obtained on an annual basis together with the latest annual accounts (either from Companies' House or directly from the customer). Both documents to be reviewed.

- A trading history review to be undertaken annually to review for performance against credit limits and terms of payments.

- Annual review of usage of the customer's credit limit to ensure that an outdated credit limit is not in existence. This is particularly important where the trade with the customer has reduced over the past year.

Credit terms

- Standard terms are 30 days from invoice. Any extension to be authorised by the Finance Director.

- A 2% settlement discount to be offered to all accounts with a profit margin of 50% or greater, or with a profit margin of 30% and a value in excess of £50,000 or with the credit controllers discretion.

Debt collection process

- Invoices to be despatched on day of issue, (day of issue to be no more than 2 days after date of delivery).

- Statements to be despatched in the second week of the month.

- Aged trade receivable analysis to be produced and reviewed on a weekly basis.

- Reminder letter to be sent once an account is overdue.

- Telephone chaser for accounts 15 days overdue.

- Customer on stop list if no payment is received within 5 days of the telephone chaser. Computerised sales order processing system updated and automatic email sent to the customer contact and the account manager (sales person).

- Letter threatening legal action if payment not received within 30 days of the first letter

- Legal proceedings / debt collection agency instructed subject to the approval of the Finance Director.

- Prepare a report suggesting an appropriate provision for bad or doubtful debts.

If at any stage in the process the customer is declared insolvent or bankrupt then contact the insolvency practitioner in order to register the debt and notify the financial accountant so that the VAT can be reclaimed.

5 External sources of information

5.1 Trade references

Traditionally, creditworthiness has been checked by asking the customer to supply trade references from **two other suppliers**. As it can be assumed that customers will not quote suppliers likely to give a bad report, it is **unwise to rely on this procedure alone**. Beware of companies that pay their two referee suppliers promptly, but pay all other suppliers late. Used in conjunction with other information, this procedure however may be helpful.

Trade reference requests should be made **formally** and should ask for credit terms. Often a standard form can be used requesting:

- the exact name of the potential customer
- the usual credit terms offered
- the expected level of business
- names and addresses of two trade referees.

From this information, the credit manager can contact the trade referees and ensure the potential customer can pay on time and adhere to agreed credit terms.

 Example

You are the credit controller for John James Ltd and you are considering a request from Donald & Sons who wish to trade on credit with your company. You are considering offering them a credit limit of £20,000 with payment terms of payment within 30 days of the invoice date. You have a standard form for trade references and Donald & Sons have provided you with the name and address of another supplier of theirs, Priory Trading, to whom you have sent the standard trade reference form. The reply you receive is given below.

What, if any, conclusions could you draw from the trade reference?

John James Ltd
4 The Parade
York
YK4 6TP

PRIVATE AND CONFIDENTIAL
Credit Controller
Priory Trading
44 Kiln Terrace
York YK3 4XS   10 May 20X5

Dear Sir or Madam

We recently received a request from Donald & Sons, a customer of ours, who gave yourselves as a reference. I would be grateful if you could assist us by answering the following questions and returning them in the stamped addressed envelope provided.

1   How long have Donald & Sons been trading with you?

     2 years   months

2   When Donald & Sons opened an account with you, did the company supply you with suitable trade and credit references?

     YES / (NO)

3   What are your normal credit terms for Donald & Sons?

     Amount: £10,000

     Terms: Cash   Weekly   (Monthly)   Other

4   Does Donald & Sons make payments in accordance with your terms?

     (YES) / NO / SLOW PAYER

5   Have you ever had to suspend credit facilities to Donald & Sons?

     YES / (NO)

     If Yes, when?

6   Please supply any other information which you consider relevant.

Thank you for your help.

Yours faithfully

B Down

B Down
Brian Down Credit Controller Solution

The information provided in the trade reference looks positive in that Priory Trading offer monthly payment terms which appear to have been adhered to. However, the amount of credit they offer is only £10,000 whereas Donald & Sons have applied to you for credit of £20,000.

However, in conjunction with perhaps another trade reference and other internal and external information about Donald & Sons, this trade reference may give you some confidence in the company.

5.2 Bank references

It is usual to take up bank references at the same time as trade references. Requests to the bank need to be **precise**; detailing the **amount of credit** you envisage giving the customer and the **credit period**. Bank replies are usually structured in one of three ways:

(1) an **unqualified**, **positive** assurance

(2) a **general indication** that the firm is operating normally

(3) a **guarded statement**, indicating that 'capital is fully employed' or 'we are unable to speak for your figures'.

It is always useful to speak to the bank on the telephone as more information may be conveyed via word of mouth. However, a reference of the latter type should put the credit manager on guard.

 Example

You are the credit controller for John James Ltd and you are considering a request from Donald & Sons who wish to trade on credit with your company. You are considering offering them a credit limit of £20,000 with payment terms of payment within 30 days of the invoice date.

You have written to Donald & Sons' bank, Northern Bank, asking for a reference having specified that you are considering a credit limit of £20,000. The bank's reply is given below.

What, if any, conclusions could you draw from the bank reference?

Northern Bank plc

Doncaster Branch
501 High Street
Doncaster DN3 4XL

Credit Controller
John James Ltd
4 The Parade
York YK4 6TP

19 May 20X5

Dear Sir or Madam

Reference: Donald & Sons

I refer to your letter dated 10 May 20X5 enquiring about the creditworthiness of the above. In our view, Donald & Sons is reasonably constituted and should prove good for your figures.

Yours faithfully

G Donarski

Gerald Donarski
Manager

Solution

This is not the very highest quality reference that could be received from a bank, but it is fairly positive and in the absence of any other negative information should make the credit controller reasonably confident about extending credit to Donald & Sons.

 Activity 4

When taking up bank references they usually provide one of 3 types of references. Which of the following is not a standard bank reference?

A   Unqualified, positive

✓ B   Qualified, positive

C   Guarded

D   General indication

5.3　Credit agency references

Credit agencies are not covered by the Data Protection Act but by the Consumer Credit Act 1974 which actually gives stronger protection in terms of the handling of information.

One of the most widely used registers is that of Dun & Bradstreet. It summarises data for around 200,000 firms in Great Britain and Northern Ireland, including the **name, address, date of formation, nominal and issued share capital, existing mortgages and charges, proprietors and associates, credit rating** and Dun & Bradstreet rating.

The vital piece of information for the credit manager is the **credit rating** which indicates the **average amount of credit to the firm**. This helps the credit manager to assess the relative size of the proposed credit limit to the potential customer. If this is much greater than the average listed, it would be advisable to undertake further investigations.

5.4　Using credit agency reports

The usefulness of a report from an agency depends on the skill and competence of the agency. A specialised agency for the particular industry concerned can normally offer more detached information, but the credit manager needs to research the agency carefully. If he is satisfied that:

- they have experienced, trained staff,
- the report is based on up-to-date information, and
- they produce reports for other reputable firms,
- then confidence may be placed in their findings.

The questions of cost and speed of reporting should not be considered as agencies who offer low-cost reports are immediately suspect. Worthwhile reports cannot be produced cheaply and, although speed is important, it is very difficult to specify minimum reporting periods for gathering information from so many different sources.

5.5　Contents of credit agency reports

The credit manager should look for the following contents in the report on the potential customer:

- name and address; associated companies with names and addresses
- name of proprietors, partners and/or directors
- amount of authorised and issued share capital
- description of the customer's activities

- latest balance sheet and profit and loss and trading account

- a list of secured charges and mortgages

- name and address of its financial advisers, bankers

- payment pattern/experience from other suppliers

- a recommended credit limit based on the findings in the report.

5.6 Problems with credit agency reports

The problems with agency reports are as follows:

- **New companies have no track record**. It is therefore very difficult to form a judgement.

- It takes time for current information to be analysed and fed into computer/appraisal systems. It is possible for very relevant information (such as the collapse of a major customer) not to be in a report.

- Suppliers' references may be too old to be of value.

5.7 Historical financial information

Extel is a company that provides a **summary of the last three years' balance sheets and details of profits, turnover, taxation, dividends, earnings per share and equity capital for up to ten years**. The usefulness of this is that all the information is on two pages and easy to access in a filing system.

5.8 Press reports

The press provide an **up-to-date commentary** on the situation within local and national companies. If the proposed customer is a big national company, reading The Financial Times enables the credit manager to keep up-to-date with half-yearly reports, comments on the customer as well as keeping abreast of industry trends and problems. Smaller more local companies are commented upon in regional and local papers.

5.9 Trade journals

Often produced weekly or monthly, trade journals are another valuable source of information and **commentary on trends and results**.

5.10 Status reports

If a current trade receivable has a large amount outstanding a status report could be requested. A status report indicates if the **customer is able to pay** for the outstanding debt and also if there are any other issues i.e. other people chase outstanding debts.

The report will contain the following information:

- County court judgement and insolvency search
- Trade receivables address, full title
- Date of last filed accounts
- Any bankruptcy or voluntary arrangements

5.11 Credit circle reports

A credit circle is a **group of people** with a common interest for example a trade association. These people meet on a regular basis to **share information on credit related matters**, such as late payers or bad trade receivables.

This information is both useful for current credit customers – are the customers struggling to pay other debts – and potential credit customers – what is their/has their credit management been like.

6 Internal sources of information

6.1 Sales ledger information

Most companies obtain information from the sales ledger where each sale is recorded and all payments from customers are noted.

All entries in the sales ledger must be identifiable and traceable back to delivery note/payment. At the end of each month, the total trade receivables' figure in the nominal ledger should be calculated as follows.

Balance at last month end	X
Add: Net invoiced sales during month	X
Less: Cash received from trade receivables	(X)
Discounts allowed to customers	(X)
Trade receivable balance at month end	X

This balance should be reconciled to the total of the balances on the individual trade receivables' accounts in the sales ledger and any differences resolved.

Although the credit manager may not have responsibility for the production of the trade receivables' listing, he will still be concerned if it is inaccurate or does not reconcile. Effective monitoring of trade receivable balances can only occur if the accounts information is correct.

6.2 The sales ledger system

All internally-produced entries to the ledger – invoices, credit notes, receipts, contra items and journal items – must have the correct customer reference in order to be posted to the correct account. All departments who raise such items must have up-to-date lists of customer codes to avoid mistakes.

6.3 Invoices

The invoice design is also important to the credit manager. Invoices should clearly state:

(a)   customer's order number

(b)   the address to which payment should be sent (c) terms of payment

(d)   invoice number, date and customer's account number, in order to ensure speedy settlement.

6.4 Receipts

The cashier will be responsible for receiving, recording and banking cash receipts, cheques, direct debits, etc.

(a)   The daily receipts need to be entered into the computer speedily to establish the credit balance of each customer, which will dictate when the next orders can be despatched.

(b)   In large organisations, large receipts should be noted separately (e.g. amounts over £5,000) and the credit manager should be allowed to read these entries before other smaller items.

(c)   The cashier should inform the credit manager immediately of any dishonoured cheques received from customers i.e. cheques returned by the bank once they have been paid in.

(d)   Payments from customers need to be reconciled quickly and allocated promptly to each trade receivable's account within the accounting system. Delay could cause problems to go unnoticed for some time and consequently affect the cash flow.

6.5 Other management data

As well as the sales ledger system, the credit manager will keep a file of customer names and addresses. This may be kept on a computer database or in a manual card index, to suit the personal preference of the manager.

The filing system is vital to ensure up-to-date names and addresses are available. This information must be kept secure and it is advisable to restrict access to this data. Normally the information can only be amended or added to by the credit department, who likewise are responsible for issuing new account numbers.

The type of information stored would include:

(a) statement address

(b) credit limit

(c) risk category

(d) payment terms

(e) regional or branch office code.

6.6 Statements and invoices

Invoices can be produced, perhaps twice a month, requesting payment from customers. At the end of each month, it is also useful to send statements to customers to draw their attention to unpaid items and to ensure that the outstanding balance is agreed between the two parties.

Statements, like invoices, must be clear so that customers can easily see the outstanding balance due.

6.7 Sales representatives' knowledge

A company's sales representatives will have **first hand information** on existing customers and may have met or known of potential customers, all of which is useful to the credit manager.

It is beneficial to the credit manager to train the sales staff to observe and listen for information on customers' ability to pay by finding out:

- the level of activity at the factory
- the impression/competence of the customer's staff and premises
- the names of other suppliers
- future plans of the customer/client
- any other information possible

This provides more **background information to analyse** alongside other facts, though the credit manager would need to be mindful of the sales representatives' optimism!

6.8 Analysis of accounts

One of the most useful sources of external information are the **annual accounts** of the customer (if it is a company). From these, various statistics can be calculated internally to help to analyse the company's situation. However, it must be remembered that the financial accounts only give **historic data** and it is often the case that the most recent accounts available from companies are at least 12 months out of date.

Whatever accounts are produced for examination, it is necessary to **respect the confidential nature** of the documents and the credit manager must exercise due care in this regard.

- The calculations for this are looked at in more detail in the chapter 3.

6.9 Trading history

An overview or investigation into a **company's trading history** can be a very useful tool when deciding to grant credit or when assessing whether to extend credit terms or limits. It can show how long a company has been in operation and how well trading has been going.

6.10 Aged analysis of trade receivables

Aged trade receivable analysis is used to assess the status of **current credit** customers.

 Definition

The aged analysis of trade receivables analyses the **balance due** from each trade receivable according to the amount of time that each individual invoice has been outstanding.

The credit manager should closely monitor the collection of debts. The aged trade receivable analysis allows speedy perusal of old/slow paying trade receivables which facilitates prompt action.

The report is usually produced at the **end of each month** alongside the monthly statements. It splits the total outstanding balance into differing age categories, for example:

(a) amounts less than one month old

(b) amounts between one and two months old

(c) amounts between two and three months old

(d) amounts over three months old.

It is also useful to print the customer's credit limit alongside this information.

The credit manager should be aware of customer who:

(a) are building up a significant outstanding account i.e. are slow payers

(b) have exceeded their credit limit

(c) have not paid for a long period of time

(d) have a strange pattern in their payments i.e. recent debts are cleared but there is an older outstanding amount.

 Activity 5

In gathering credit information on a potential client you would use both internal sources of credit information and external sources of credit information. Which of the following is an example of internal information?

A   Trade references

B   Sales representatives knowledge

C   Credit agency

D   Bank references

7   Summary

In this chapter we have considered the question of whether to grant credit to a customer and how much credit to grant.

The decision as to whether to grant credit should be based upon external information such as references and also internal information created from ratio analysis of a customer's financial statements. After all of this information has been considered, a final decision can be made as to whether or not to grant the customer credit terms.

Answers to chapter activities

 Activity 1

Answer D

 Activity 2

Answer C

The supplier gains 60 days' use of the amount due at a cost of 5%, i.e. an annual rate of:

$(5/(100-5)) \times (365/(90-30)) \times 100 = 32\%$.

This discount rate is unlikely to be worthwhile in the UK.

 Activity 3

Answer A

£350 × 98.5% = £344.75

$(1.5/98.5) \times (365/(60-40)) \times 100 = 12.1\%$

 Activity 4

Answer B

 Activity 5

Answer B

8 Test your knowledge

Workbook Activity 6

Which of the following is not a reason for companies offering credit terms to their customers?

✓ A   To reduce expenses

B   To increase sales

C   To improve cash flow   ✓

D   To improve customer relations

Workbook Activity 7

A company is concerned about the size of its trade receivables and its cash flows. It therefore decides to offer a 'prompt payment discount' of 3% for payment within 10 days. Without the discount, customers take 45 days' credit.

What is the amount the customer would pay on an invoice of £4,000 and what is the simple annual interest rate of the discount?

A   £3,880 and 112.9%

B   £3,880 and 18.8%

✓ C   £3,880 and 32.3%

D   £3,880 and 310.0%

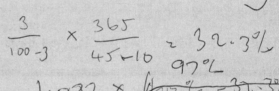

Workbook Activity 8

Salon Select Limited supplies hairdressing consumables to the hairdressing business in Scotland and North East England from its base in Glasgow. Salon Select has been approached by Crocodile Cuts, which operates a chain of hairdressers, to supply goods for its five shops. Crocodile Cuts has asked for credit of £20,000 on 60 days' terms and has supplied a bank reference and two trade references. You have written to the bank and the trade referees and their responses are enclosed.

Strathclyde Bank plc

Argyle Street Branch
501 Argyle Street
Glasgow G2 7LT

Credit Controller
Salon Select Limited
1 Weaver Street
Glasgow GI 9OP
19 May 20X5

Dear Sir or Madam,

Reference: Crocodile Cuts Limited

I refer to your letter dated 10 May 20X5 enquiring about the creditworthiness of the above. In our view, Crocodile Cuts is reasonably constituted and should prove good for your figures.

Yours faithfully

G Donarski

Gerald Donarski
Manager

Salon Select Limited
1 Weaver Street
Glasgow
G1 9OP

PRIVATE AND CONFIDENTIAL
Credit Controller
Black Fred - The Barber's Friend Limited
27 Westminster Terrace
Glasgow G3 4EF   10 May 20X5

Dear Sir or Madam

We recently received a request from Crocodile Cuts Limited, a customer of ours, who gave yourselves as a reference. I would be grateful if you could assist us by answering the following questions and returning them in the stamped addressed envelope provided.

1   How long have Crocodile Cuts been trading with you?

      2 years months

2   When Crocodile Cuts opened an account with you, did the company supply you with suitable trade and credit references?

YES / (NO)

3   What are your normal credit terms for Crocodile Cuts?

Amount: £10,000

Terms: Cash Weekly (Monthly) Other (please detail below)

4   Does Crocodile Cuts make payments in accordance with your terms?

(YES) / NO / SLOW PAYER

5   Have you ever had to suspend credit facilities to Crocodile Cuts?

(YES) / NO

If YES, when?

6   Please supply any other information which you consider relevant. Thank you for your help.

Yours faithfully

B Diamond

Bruce Diamond
Credit Controller

Salon Select Limited
1 Weaver Street
Glasgow
G1 9OP

PRIVATE AND CONFIDENTIAL
Credit Controller
19 St Mary's Court
Hyndland, Glasgow G11 7UN   10 May 20X5

Dear Sir or Madam

We recently received a request from Crocodile Cuts Limited, a customer of ours, who gave yourselves as a reference. I would be grateful if you could assist us by answering the following questions and returning them in the stamped addressed envelope provided.

1   How long have Crocodile Cuts been trading with you?

    3 years   months

2　　When Crocodile Cuts opened an account with you, did the company supply you with suitable trade and credit references?

YES　/　(NO)

3　　What are your normal credit terms for Crocodile Cuts?

Amount: N/A

Terms: Cash Weekly (Monthly) Other (please detail below)

4　　Does Crocodile Cuts make payments in accordance with your terms?

YES　/　NO　/　SLOW PAYER　N/A

5　　Have you ever had to suspend credit facilities to Crocodile Cuts?

YES　/　NO　N/A

If YES, when?

6　　Please supply any other information which you consider relevant. Thank you for your help.

Yours faithfully

B Diamond

Bruce Diamond
Credit Controller

Study the two references above and consider Crocodile Cuts' request. Recommend to your credit manager how Salon Select should proceed.

The bank reference has given a general indication that the firm is operating normally and is not a cause for concern.

However, in one of the trade references, from Black Fred, it has been advised that is has been necessary to suspend credit facilities to Crocodile Cuts. Black Fred has also confirmed that they offer a credit limit of £10,000 to Croc.Cuts whereas they have requested a credit limit of £20,000.

I would recommend to the credit Manager that credit limit of £10,000 should be offered to Croc Cuts for a 6 month period at which time the credit limit should be revised

Analysis of credit information

Introduction

In this chapter we shall consider the analysis of the information we gathered in chapter 2 and how the data can be analysed to assess the risk of offering credit to potential credit customers or extending credit facilities of current customers.

KNOWLEDGE

Identify the information requirements for credit control (2.2)

Explain methods of analysing credit control information including: age analysis; average periods of credit given and received; incidence of bad and doubtful debts (2.4)

Identify a range of methods of analysing information on trade receivables (2.5)

SKILLS

Evaluate the current credit status of customers and potential customers (1.1)

Agree changes to credit levels or credit terms with customers (1.4)

Regularly monitor and analyse information relating to trade receivables' accounts (2.1)

Promptly send information regarding significant outstanding accounts and potential bad debts to relevant individuals within the organisation (2.2)

CONTENTS

1 Analysis of trade receivables
2 Key performance indicators

1 Analysis of trade receivables

1.1 Introduction

There are variously sources of information that can be used to analyse trade receivables most of these have been discussed in the previous chapter.

When analysing current credit customers you may need to decide on which customers to focus the debt collection efforts on and also to assess the riskiness of having companies continue as trade receivables or expand credit facilities offered to them.

When deciding whether or not to grant credit to a customer you will need to be able to analyse any information gathered.

Some of the techniques mentioned are more useful for current credit customers, some for potential credit customers and some are more useful for analysing both.

Current credit customers	Potential credit customers	Current and potential credit customers
Aged trade receivable analysis	Trade references	Credit circle reports
80/20 rule	Bank references	Performance indicators
Materiality		Trading history
Sales ledger information		Credit rating agencies
		Press reports
		Trade journals
		Status reports
		Sale representatives knowledge

1.2 80/20 rule

Analysis of trade receivables can be simplified using Parento's Principle or the 80/20 rule. Vilfredo Parento noted that 20% of the people in Italy owned 80% of the country's wealth.

If this principle is applied to the trade receivables of a company it could help the credit manager **focus the credit control team**. The credit manager could assume that **80% of the debts owed** in value were **due to only 20% of the customer accounts** thereby focusing attention and analysis on these 20% of customers.

KAPLAN PUBLISHING

1.3 Materiality

Another way to assess trade receivables is on the materiality of the debt or the value of debt in comparison to total value of trade receivables. If one debt is the **majority** of the trade receivables then attentions needs to be focused on receiving that money.

The credit manager also needs to consider the **cost of collecting** the debt in comparison to the value of the debt. A small outstanding amount may cost more to collect than it is actually worth to the business.

 Activity 1

Which of the following is not a method of analysing credit control information?

A ✓ Aged trade payable analysis

B   Parento's Principle

C   Key performance indicators

D   Trading history

 Activity 2

Which of the following information should be used to assess the credit status of a new customer?

(i)   Aged trade receivable analysis

(ii)   Draft contract for trade

(iii)   Trade references ✓

(iv)   Bank references ✓

(v)   Financial accounts ✓

(vi)   Copies of outstanding invoices

A   All of the above

B   (iii) only

C ✓ (iii), (iv) and (v) only

D   (ii) and (v) only

Activity 3

Which of the following would be used to assess the credit status of a current customer?

(i) ✓ Aged trade receivable analysis

(ii) Draft contract for trade

(iii) Trade references

(iv) Bank references

(v) ✓ Financial accounts

(vi) ✓ Copies of outstanding invoices

A (i) only

B ✓ (i), (v) and (vi) only

C (v) and (vi) only

D All of the above

---

2 Key performance indicators

2.1 Key performance indicators

Key performance indicators can be calculated to analyse financial accounts provided by a business. There are three aspects of a company's performance that the credit manager should consider.

- **Solvency** – the ability of the company to pay its debts from its current assets, i.e. there are sufficient liquid resources.

- **Profitability** – this is obviously important as, in the long run, an unprofitable company will not survive.

- **Gearing or capital ratios** – these are concerned with the ratio of risk capital (equity) to loan capital.

This information can be used to decide on **whether to offer credit terms** to a company or where to **extend credit terms** to a current credit customer. With current credit customers it is also a useful tool to be able to **assess how the business is progressing** – have ratios improved or worsened. This could lead to a **change in credit policy** being implemented.

Before examining the various accounting ratios in detail, it is important to remember that:

(a)   an opinion cannot be formed from one year's statistics alone – it is more useful to develop trends for several years/months before concluding;

(b)   it is helpful to be able to compare the company's statistics with other companies in the same industrial sector – hopefully the company concerned will be better than average;

(c)   the accounts may be distorted due to inter-company transactions, group funding etc and so an opinion can only be formed by looking at the accounts for the whole group;

(d)   statistics are only statistics! It is very easy in recessionary or inflationary times for the position of a company to change very quickly from profitable to loss making, so the credit manager must not become blinded by numbers alone.

2.2   Liquidity/Solvency ratios

Current ratio

This is a common method of analysing working capital (net current assets) and is generally accepted as the measure of **short-term solvency**. It indicates the extent to which the claims of short-term trade payables are covered by assets that are expected to be converted to cash in a period roughly corresponding to the maturity of the claims.

$$\text{Current ratio} \quad = \quad \frac{\text{Current assets}}{\text{Current Liabilities}}$$

The aim is to ensure that current liabilities can be met as they fall due. Sometimes, textbooks suggest that if a business's current ratio is below a certain level (which is usually given as between 1.5 and 2), the business should become seriously concerned. This should not be taken to be a strict rule, because:

(a)   current liabilities include the bank overdraft which, in practice, is not repayable within one year (technically, of course, repayable on demand)

(b)   different types of industry will have different typical current ratios. For example a supermarket will have high payable levels and high inventories but very few trade receivables; whereas a manufacturing business will not only have high payable and inventory levels but also significant levels of trade receivables.

Acid test ratio

Known as the **quick ratio**, this is calculated in the same way as for the current ratio but inventories are excluded from current assets.

$$\text{Acid test ratio} \quad = \quad \frac{\text{Current assets} - \text{inventory}}{\text{Current liabilities}}$$

This ratio is a much better test of the **immediate solvency** of a business because of the length of time necessary to convert inventory into cash (via sales and trade receivables).

Although increasing liquid resources more usually indicate favourable trading, it could be that funds are not being used to their best advantage (e.g. a large unused cash balance).

Receivable days

Also known as the trade receivables' ratio

$$\text{Average collection period} = \frac{\text{Receivable s}}{\text{Turnover}} \times 365$$

This indicates the time scale over which the **company receives cash from its credit customers**. This is not directly relevant to the decision whether or not to grant credit but it can give useful information about how the company operates.

Payable days

Also known as the trade payables' ratio

$$\text{Average payment period} = \frac{\text{Payables}}{\text{Cost of sales}} \times 365$$

This is **directly relevant** to the decision whether or not to grant credit as it indicates the general time scale over which the **company pays its current credit suppliers.**

It is desirable for the trade receivables' collection period to be shorter than the trade payables' payment period. This way the company collects what is due before it has to pay out to its own trade payables. However, with a competitive market it is not always possible to arrange the cash flows so advantageously. Nevertheless, the ratios should not be too different to avoid a negative cash flow.

Be aware with both the above ratios as:

- Accounts do not show the split between cash and credit sales/purchases. This means that assumptions have to be made (e.g. all sales on credit, cost of sales represents the credit purchases) that may distort the result.

- Seasonality may also distort the result.

Inventory turnover

This ratio indicates whether a business's inventories are justified in relation to its sales. If inventory turnover falls in terms of number of times or increases in terms of number of days, this may indicate excess inventories or sluggish sales.

$$\text{Inventory turnover (in days)} = \frac{\text{Inventory}}{\text{Cost of sales}} \times 365$$

$$\text{Inventory turnover (no. of times)} = \frac{\text{Cost of sales}}{\text{Inventory}}$$

Working capital cycle

Inventory turnover days + Receivable days – Payable days

This indicator uses the above formulae to work out how long it takes to convert inventory, trade receivables and trade payables into cash. The longer the cycle the longer it takes to convert inventory, trade receivables into cash to pay the trade payables.

2.3   Profitability ratios

Return on capital employed (return on assets)

Capital employed is normally measured as **equity plus non-current liabilities** (or, alternatively, **non-current assets plus current assets minus current liabilities**); it represents the long-term investment in the business.

Return on capital employed is frequently regarded as the **best measure** of profitability, indicating how successful a business is in utilising its assets. This ratio is only meaningful when the true values of assets are known and used in the formula.

$$\text{Return on capital employed} = \frac{\text{Profit before interest and taxation}}{\text{Capital employed}} \times 100$$

A low return on capital employed is caused by either a low profit margin or a low asset turnover or both.

The aim is to see how effectively the business is using the money invested in it.

Care should be taken with the interpretation of this ratio for the following reasons:

- it is based upon the statement of financial position values of the net assets rather than the true market value

- as the statement of financial position values are based upon historical cost then the age structure of the assets of the business can also affect the return on capital employed.

- often new investment does not bring immediate profits. This may be for a number of reasons. It may take time for the company's employees to learn how to use the new equipment. Alternatively it may take the company time to obtain enough orders to use the new facilities to the full. (This may result in a temporary reduction in the ROCE.)

Net profit margin

$$\text{Margin} = \frac{\text{Net profit before interest and taxation}}{\text{Turnover}} \times 100$$

A low margin indicates low selling prices or high costs or both. Comparative analysis will reveal the level of prices and costs in relation to competitors.

Gross profit margin

This ratio isolates the pure 'nuts and bolts' of a business, i.e. ignoring indirect expenses and sundry income.

$$\text{Margin} = \frac{\text{Gross profit}}{\text{Turnover}} \times 100$$

A low margin indicates a similar position to a low net profit margin, but the causes can be traced more readily to trends in sales and cost of sales.

Looking at these two ratios together can determine whether a fall in the gross profit margin can be explained by a misclassification of cost rather than by deteriorating trade success.

	20X1 £	20X0 £
Turnover	100	100
Cost of sales	(85)	(80)
Gross profit	15	20
Overheads	(5)	(10)
Net profit	10	10
GPM	15%	20%
NPM	10%	10%

The fact that the net profit margin has remained constant while the gross profit margin has fallen would lead us to check that our costs had been properly classified.

This is an illustration of using more than one ratio to guide our thoughts.

Asset turnover

This will show how fully a company is **utilising its assets**.

$$\text{Asset turnover} = \frac{\text{Turnover}}{\text{Capital employed}}$$

A low turnover shows that a company is not generating a sufficient volume of business for the size of the asset investment. This may be remedied by increasing sales or by disposing of some of the assets or both.

Interest cover

This measures the ratio of the profit before interest to the interest charge itself.

$$\text{Interest cover} = \frac{\text{Profit before interest}}{\text{Interest charge}}$$

This gives an indication of how easily the company can maintain payments of its loan and debenture interest and therefore gives additional information about the riskiness of the company.

The purpose of the assessment of the customer's financial statements is to determine the likelihood that they will pay their trade debts on time. If a company has long-term loan capital in its capital structure, then the interest on this must be paid thereby reducing the profits available to make other payments such as those to trade payables. Therefore the interest cover is additional evidence of the risk associated with the company.

2.4 Debt ratios

Gearing ratio

Here we are trying to assess the amount of long-term capital in the company's capital structure as this can be an element of the riskiness of a company.

$$\text{Borrowing ratio (gearing ratio)} = \frac{\text{total debt}}{\text{total debt} + \text{equity}} \times 100$$

There are different versions of the gearing ratio calculation:

- as above or,

- $\dfrac{\text{total debt}}{\text{equity}} \times 100$

- total debt could mean long and short term debt or just long term debt
- in the exam make sure you check to see what is being used

The greater the extent to which a company is financed by debt, the greater is the risk of investing in it.

From a lender's point of view, the more debt there is, the less likely that money will be recovered if the company goes into liquidation.

From a shareholder's point of view, the more debt there is, the greater the variability of return.

2.5 Cash flow ratios

The most important asset for a company to have to be able to meet its debt requirement is cash. The following calculations are similar to some of the ones above but the net income figure is adjusted for values that are calculated due to accounting concepts.

Earnings before interest, tax, depreciation and amortisation (EBITDA) – is net income but with accounting concepts such as accruals, depreciation removed to give an indication of cash flow.

EBITDA interest cover

$$\text{Interest cover} = \frac{\text{EBITDA}}{\text{Interest paid}}$$

EBITDA to total debt

$$= \frac{\text{EBITDA}}{\text{Total debt}}$$

Both these formulae give indication of how cash relates to the expenditure requirements if a business.

2.6 Examples

Example

The following illustration demonstrates some of the ratios with which you need to be familiar when assessing credit risk.

Summarised statement of financial position at 31 December 20X1

	£000	£000
Non-current assets, at cost, less depreciation		2,600
Current assets		
Inventory	600	
Trade receivables	900	
Balance at bank	100	
	1,600	
Trade payables	(800)	
		800
		3,400
Non-current liabililties:		
Loan		(1,400)
		2,000
Equity		
Ordinary share capital (£1 shares)		1,000
Preference share capital		200
Retained earnings		800
		2,000

Summarised income statement for the year ended 31 December 20X1

	20X1 £000
Revenue	6,000
Cost of sales	(4,000)
Gross profit	2,000
Operating expenses	(1,660)
Net trading profit	340
Finance cost	(74)
Profit before tax	266
Taxation	(106)
	160
Preference dividend	(10)
Profit available for ordinary shareholders	150

Note that cost of sales and operating expenses include £600,000 of depreciation charges.

Solution

Solvency ratios

- **Current ratio**

$$\text{Current ratio} = \frac{\text{Current assets}}{\text{Current liabilities}} = \frac{£1,600}{£800} = 2$$

- **Acid test ratio**

$$\text{Current ratio} = \frac{\text{Current assets - inventory}}{\text{Current liabilities}} = \frac{£1,600 - 600}{£800} = 1.25$$

- **Receivable days**

$$\text{Average collection period} = \frac{\text{Receivables}}{\text{Turnover}} \times 365 = \frac{£900}{£6,000} \times 365 = 55 \text{ days}$$

- **Payable days**

$$\text{Average payment period} = \frac{\text{Payables}}{\text{Cost of sales}} \times 365 = \frac{£800}{£4,000} \times 365 = 73 \text{ days}$$

- **Inventory turnover**

Inventory turnover =

$$\frac{\text{Inventory}}{\text{Cost of Sales}} \times 365 = \frac{600}{4,000} \times 365 = 55 \text{ days}$$

Inventory turnover $= \dfrac{\text{Cost of sales}}{\text{Inventory}} = \dfrac{£4,000}{£600} = 6.67 \text{ times}$

- **Working Capital cycle**

Inventory days + Receivable days – Payable days

$$= 55 + 55 - 73 = 37 \text{ days}$$

Profitability ratios

- **Gross profit margin**

$$\text{Margin} = \frac{\text{Gross profit}}{\text{Turnover}} \times 100$$

$$= \frac{£2,000}{£6,000} \times 100 = 33.33\%$$

- **Net profit margin (on sales)**

$$\text{Margin} = \frac{\text{Net profit before interest and taxation}}{\text{Turnover}} \times 100$$

$$= \frac{£340}{£6,000} \times 100 = 5.67\%$$

- **Return on capital employed (return on assets)**

$$\text{Return on capital employed} = \frac{\text{Profit before interest and taxation}}{\text{Capital employed}} \times 100$$

$$= \frac{£340}{£2,000 + 1,400} \times 100 = 10\%$$

- **Asset turnover**

$$\text{Asset turnover} = \frac{\text{Turnover}}{\text{Capital employed}} = \frac{£6,000}{£3,400} = 1.76 \text{ times}$$

- **Interest cover**

$$\text{Interest cover} = \frac{\text{Profit before interest}}{\text{Interest charge}} = \frac{£340}{£74} = 4.6 \text{ times}$$

Gearing ratio

$$\text{Borrowing ratio (gearing ratio)} = \frac{\text{Total debt}}{\text{Capital employed}} \times 100$$

$$= \frac{£1,400}{£2,000 + 1,400} \times 100 = 41\%$$

Activity 4

Summarised statement of financial position at 31 December 20X1

	£000	£000	£000
Non-current assets, at cost, less depreciation			2,500
Current assets			
Inventorys		900	
Trade receivables		800	
Balance at bank		300	
		2,000	
Current liabilities			
Trade trade payables	700		
Accrued charges	300		
		(1,000)	
			1,000
			3,500
Non-current liabilities			
10% debentures (loan)			(1,500)
			2,000
Capital and reserves			
Ordinary shares (£1 shares)			1,000
Preference shares			250
General reserve		600	
Income statement		150	
			750
			2,000

Income statement for year ended 31 December 20X1

	£000	£000
Turnover		6,000
Cost of sales		
Inventory at 1 January	500	
Purchases	4,000	
	4,500	
Less: inventory at 31 December 20X1	(900)	
		(3,600)
Gross profit		2,400
Administrative expenses and distribution costs		(1,830)
Trading profit		570
Debenture interest		(150)
Profit before tax		420
Taxation		(210)
		210
Preference dividend		(10)
Profit available for ordinary shareholders		200

Required

Calculate as many useful ratios as possible from the information above.

As mentioned earlier in the chapter one set of performance indicator calculations is not really enough to draw conclusions from. Many companies will request a couple of years of accounts to perform calculations on to see how the business under investigation has changed.

Another method is to have a credit rating (scoring) system to be able to grade a company's credit risk.

Activity 5

The accounts of Falcon Limited for the years ended 30 June 20X3 and 30 June 20X2 are as follows.

Statement of financial position

	20X3		20X2	
	£	£	£	£
Non-current assets				
Property		125,000		75,000
Plant		130,000		70,000
		255,000		145,000
Current assets				
Inventory	120,000		100,000	
Trade receivables	80,000		60,000	
	200,000		160,000	
Current liabilities				
Trade payables	45,000		30,000	
Overdraft	15,000		5,000	
Taxation	20,000		15,000	
	80,000		50,000	
Net current assets		120,000		110,000
		375,000		255,000
Non-current liabilities				
7% Loan		(50,000)		(50,000)
		325,000		205,000
Capital and reserves				
£1 ordinary shares		100,000		50,000
Share premium account		90,000		35,000
Income statement		135,000		120,000
		325,000		205,000

Income statement

	20X3 £	20X2 £
Turnover	525,000	425,000
Trading profit	53,500	41,000
Interest	(3,500)	(3,500)
Profit before tax	50,000	37,500
Tax	(20,000)	(15,000)
Profit after tax	30,000	22,500
Dividends	(15,000)	(10,000)
Retained profit	15,000	12,500

Credit rating (scoring) system	Score
Operating profit margin	
losses	-5
less than 5%	0
5% and above but less than 10%	5
10% and above but less than 20%	10
more than 20%	20
Interest cover	
no cover	-30
less than 1	-20
more than 1 but less than 2	-10
more than 2 but less than 4	0
more than 4	10
Liquidity ratio	
less than 1	-20
between 1 and 1.25	-10

between 1.25 and 1.5	0
above 1.5	10
Gearing (total debt/(total debt plus equity))	
less than 25%	20
25% and above but less than 50%	10
more than 50% less than 65%	0
between 65% and 75%	-20
between 75% and 80%	-40
above 80%	-100
Risk	**aggregate score**
very low risk	Between 60 and 21
low risk	Between 20 and 1
medium risk	Between 0 and -24
high risk	Between -25 and -50
very high risk	Above -50

Required

Calculate the performance indicators listed below and using the credit rating system calculate the risk of having Falcon Limited as a payable

	Indicator	Rating	Indicator	Rating
Year	20X3		20X2	
Operating profit margin	18.19%	10	9.65%	5
Interest cover	14.3X	10	11.7	10
Current ratio	2.5:1	20	3.2:1	10
Gearing	13.3%	20	19.6%	20
Total		60		65

Activity 6

Jacket and Tie have been trading with your company for several years and has, until recently, always paid to terms. Recently there have been a couple of late payments and Jacket and Tie have contacted you asking to increase their credit limit from £50,000 to £75,000.

Jacket and Tie have supplied the accounts below:

Income statement	2008 £	2009 £
Turnover	350,000	230,000
Cost of sales	(227,500)	(149,500)
Gross profit	122,500	80,500
Distribution costs	(25,000)	(20,000)
Administration costs	(50,000)	(45,000)
Operating profit	47,500	15,500
Interest paid	(5,000)	(5,000)
Profit before tax	42,500	10,500
Tax	(6,000)	(5,000)
Profit after tax	36,500	5,500

Statement of financial position	2008 £	2009 £
Non-current assets	150,000	30,000
Current assets		
Inventory	25,690	18,164
Trade receivables	62,789	41,918
Cash	35,878	500
	124,357	60,582

Current liabilities		
Short term loan	21,959	
Trade payable	23,980	18,164
	45,939	18,164
Net current assets	78,418	42,418
Long term loans	15,000	50,000
Net assets	213,418	22,418
Represented by		
Share capital	100	100
Revaluation reserve	160,000	
Profit and loss account	53,318	22,318
	213,418	22,418

Jacket and Tie have also provided you with some further information:

We have recently succeeded in securing the business of several new large clients so we have had to purchase new assets with a long term loan to ensure that we can meet demand

We expect sales to continue to increase next year but for our costs to stay constant as we are able to reduce variable costs through the use of our new machines.

Using the template provided:

1   Calculate the key indicators for the current and previous years for Jacket and Tie

2   Rate the company using the credit rating (scoring system) provided below.

Credit rating (scoring) system	Score
Operating profit margin	
losses	-5
less than 5%	0
5% and above but less than 10%	5

10% and above but less than 20%	10
more than 20%	20
Interest cover	
no cover	-30
less than 1	-20
more than 1 but less than 2	-10
more than 2 but less than 4	0
more than 4	10
Liquidity ratio	
less than 1	-20
between 1 and 1.25	-10
between 1.25 and 1.5	0
above 1.5	10
Gearing (total debt/(total debt plus equity))	
less than 25%	20
25% and above but less than 50%	10
more than 50% less than 65%	0
between 65% and 75%	-20
between 75% and 80%	-40
above 80%	-100
Risk	**aggregate score**
very low risk	Between 60 and 21
low risk	Between 20 and 1
medium risk	Between 0 and -24
high risk	Between -25 and -50
very high risk	Above -50

Jacket and Tie	Indicator 2008	Rating	Indicator 2009	Rating
Operating profit margin	13.6% ✓ 10 ✓		67.4% 6.7 20	15
Interest cover	9.5 ✓ 10 ✓		3.1 ✓	0
Current ratio	2 1.0.58 × 420	10	3.2 1.7 ×	10
Gearing	14 86.57%	20 ×	69.0%	-20
Trade receivable days	65 ✓		66	
Trade payable days	38 ✓		44	
Total rating		20		15

v.l.r. 50   m.r. -5 10

3 Based on the results and the other information available recommend, with reasons, a course of action

The credit rating for Jacket and Tie has gone from being very low risk in 2008 to medium risk in 2009 which is a cause for concern especially as the co. now wishes to increase its credit limit to £75,000.

However, Jacket and Tie have been investing heavily in assets, secured by a long term loan, that it hopes will enable the co. to meet the demand of new customers.

The securing of these assets accounts with a loan for the greater risk that is evidenced by the significantly increased gearing ratio in 2009 and lower interest cover in 2009.

On balance, my company should grant the increase in credit limit to £75,000 as Jacket and Tie has had a history of trading with us for several years, always paying to terms, and it would be bad for the business to lose such an important customer. However, trading on credit with Jacket and Tie should be closely monitored going forward.

KAPLAN PUBLISHING

3 Summary

Key performance indicators would be the most useful for analysing potential credit customers but it should not be used in isolation.

Answers to chapter activities

Activity 1

Answer A

Activity 2

Answer C

Activity 3

Answer B

Activity 4

Possible ratios – if you have calculated any others check with your tutor.

Return on capital employed✓	(570 / 3,500) × 100	= 16.3%
Net profit on sales ✓	(570 / 6,000) × 100	= 9.5%
Asset turnover	6,000 / 3,500	= 1.7 times
Current ratio ✓	2,000 / 1,000	= 2:1
Acid test ratio ✓	1,100 / 1,000	= 1.1:1
Inventory to net current assets	(900 / 1,000) × 100	= 90%
Receivable days ✓	(800 / 6,000) × 365	= 49 days
Payable days ✓	(700 / 3,600) × 365	= 71 days
Rate of inventory turnover ✓	3,600 / 900	= 4 times
Gearing ratio (including preference shares)	((1,500 + 250) / 3,500) × 100	= 50%

Interest cover (including preference divi)	570 / (150 + 10)	= 3.6 times

 Activity 5

Operating Profit margin

20X3	20X2
(53,500/ 525,000) × 100 = 10.19%	(41,000 / 425,000) × 100 = 9.65%

Interest Cover

20X3	20X2
53500/5300 = 10.1 times	41,000/3,000 = 11.7 times

Current ratio

20X3	20X2
200,000 / 80,000 = 2.5	160,000 / 50,000 = 3.2

Gearing ratio

20X3	20X2
(50,000 / 375,000) × 100 = 13.33%	(50,000 / 255,000) × 100 = 19.6%

	Indicator	Rating	Indicator	Rating
Year	20X3		20X2	
Operating profit margin	10.19%	5	9.64%	5
Interest cover	10.1	10	11.7	10
Current ratio	2.5	10	3.2	10
Gearing	13.33%	20	19.6%	20
Total		45		45

Falcon Limited is very low risk and should be allowed credit terms.

Activity 6

Jacket and Tie	Indicator 2008	Rating	Indicator 2009	Rating
Operating profit margin	13.6%	10	6.7%	5
Interest cover	9.5	10	3.1	0
Current ratio	2.7	10	3.3	10
Gearing	14.8%	20	69%	-20
Trade receivable days	65.5		66.5	
Trade payable days	38.5		44.3	
Total rating		50		-5

Workings for Indicators

Indicator	2008	2009
Operating profit margin	47,500/350,000 × 100	15,500/230,000 × 100
Interest cover	47,500/5,000	15,500/5,000
Current ratio	124,357/45,939	60,582/18,164
Gearing	(15,000+21,959)/ (213,418+15,000+21,959) × 100	50,000/(22,418+50,000) × 100
Trade receivable days	62,789/350,000 × 365	41,918/230,000 × 365
Trade payable days	23,980/227,500 × 365	18,164/149,500 × 365

Jacket and Tie's credit rating has reduce over the time period above and have gone from very low risk 2008 to medium risk in 2009. Jacket and Tie have been trading with us for a number of years and has always met terms until recently. The main cause of the credit rating change in the level of gearing the company now has – this can be explained by the increase in the loan allowed by the bank. The loan would also explain the drop in interest cover. The company remain liquid and are maintaining adequate trade receivable and trade payable day ratios.

It may be worth asking for some form of security if we are going to extend credit terms – i.e. retention of title clause in the contract.

4 Test your knowledge

 Workbook Activity 7

A new customer, Crust Limited, has asked your company for credit terms. Your company has a policy of carrying out an analysis of a customer's financial statements as a part of an internal credit checking exercise, before deciding whether to agree to granting credit. Crust Limited has requested a credit limit of £30,000.

You have been given the financial statements of Crust Limited (extracts shown below)

Extracts of accounts of Crust Limited

	Current year £	Previous year £
Income statement		
Turnover	3,100,000	3,350,000
Cash operating expenses	2,400,000	2,700,000
Operating profit	105,000	53,000
Interest charges	4,000	3,000
Statement of financial position		
Non-current assets	310,000	367,000
	———	———
Current assets		
Inventory	62,000	66,000
Receivables	75,000	86,000
Cash and short-term investments	30,000	8,000
	———	———
	167,000	160,000
	———	———
Current liabilities		
Bank overdraft	5,000	28,000
Trade payables	70,000	75,000
Other payables	2,000	12,000
	———	———
	77,000	115,000
	———	———

Total assets less current liabilities	400,000	412,000
Bank loans	40,000	30,000
Total assets less total liabilities	360,000	382,000
Share capital	100,000	100,000
Income statement	225,000	260,000
Retained for the year	35,000	22,000
	360,000	382,000

Credit rating (scoring) system	Score
Operating profit margin	
losses	-5
less than 5%	0
5% and above but less than 10%	5
10% and above but less than 20%	10
more than 20%	20
Interest cover	
no cover	-30
less than 1	-20
more than 1 but less than 2	-10
more than 2 but less than 4	0
more than 4	10
Liquidity ratio	
less than 1	-20
between 1 and 1.25	-10
between 1.25 and 1.5	0
above 1.5	10

Gearing (total debt/(total debt plus equity))	
less than 25%	20
25% and above but less than 50%	10
more than 50% less than 65%	0
between 65% and 75%	-20
between 75% and 80%	-40
above 80%	-100

Risk	Aggregate score
very low risk	Between 60 and 21
low risk	Between 20 and 1
medium risk	Between 0 and -24
high risk	Between -25 and -50
very high risk	Above -50

Using the template provided:

1   Calculate the key indicators for the current and previous years for Crust Limited

2   Rate the company using the credit rating (scoring system) provided above.

Crust Limited	Indicator Current year	Rating	Indicator Previous year	Rating
Operating profit margin	3.4%	0	1.6%	0
Interest cover	26.3	10	17.7	10
Current ratio	2.2	10	1.4	0
Gearing	10%	20	7.3%	20
Total rating		40		30

v.l.r.   ✓   v.l.r.

3   Based on your results recommend, with reasons, whether the requested credit limit should be given to Crust Limited.

4   If credit is being refused draft a letter to Crust Limited communicating the decision and explain what action the company could take to improve its chance of being granted credit in the future. If credit is being allowed prepare a telephone script which could be used by the person contacting the company to communicate the decision.

Managing trade receivables

Introduction

In this chapter, we will consider how it is best to manage the trade receivables of a business, including how to communicate with trade receivables. We also discuss what methods are available to aid the collection of monies.

KNOWLEDGE	CONTENTS
Explain legal and administrative procedures for the collection of debts (1.4)	1 Communication with trade receivables
Explain the importance of liquidity management (2.1)	2 Refusal of credit
Identify the information requirements for credit control (2.2)	3 Payment methods
Identify a range of methods of analysing information on trade receivables (2.5)	4 Debt collection procedures
Identify a range of methods for the collection and management of debts and explain the appropriateness of each method (3.2)	5 Monitoring debt collection
	6 Factoring
	7 Invoice discounting
	8 Debt insurance
	9 Stopping supplies
	10 Collection agencies

SKILLS

Evaluate the current credit status of customers and potential customers (1.1)

Agree credit terms with customers in accordance with the organisation's policies (1.2)

Open new accounts for those customers with an established credit status (1.3)

Agree changes to credit levels or credit terms with customers (1.4)

Discuss tactfully the reasons for refusing or extending credit with customers (1.5)

Regularly monitor and analyse information relating to trade receivables' accounts (2.1)

Promptly send information regarding significant outstanding accounts and potential bad debts to relevant individuals within the organisation (2.2)

Negotiate with trade receivables in a courteous and professional manner and accurately record the outcomes of negotiations (2.3)

In accordance with organisational procedures select debt recovery methods appropriate to individual outstanding trade receivables (2.4)

Make recommendations to write off bad debts and make provisions for doubtful debts based upon a realistic analysis of all known factors (2.5)

1 Communication with trade receivables

1.1 Introduction

Once a potential trade receivable has been analysed and it has been agreed that they can be offered credit then communication with them is required regarding a number of issues.

It will be necessary to request information from the new trade receivable to be able to **set up a credit account**. This includes:

- confirmation of name
- confirmation of address
- amount they want to be able to buy on credit
- VAT registration number

It is also necessary to agree the **terms and conditions** of the credit agreement.

Other things that would be discussed include:

- if there will be a **settlement discount** for prompt or early payment
- it will be necessary to agreeing how **payment** will be made (more detail later in the chapter)
- any **legal conditions** within the contract such as 'Retention of Title'.

1.2 Methods of Communication

There are a number of ways that a company can communicate with a trade receivable. Each method may be used as part of the set up checks or as an on-going method of managing trade receivables.

Face to Face communications are required:

- if there is a big contract being formed there is likely to be a face to face meeting to discuss and agree prices and payment schedule
- if there is a query over an invoice
- to confirm the existence of the company in question

Telecommunications would include:

- telephone – useful for checking details (confirm any conversations in writing)

- email – quick method of communication, can get delivery and read receipts on emails, good for audit trail of conversations

- internet – use to display credit control policy, any price changes

Written communication would include:

- invoices – sent when goods/services delivered

- statements – sent once a month to show status of account

- letters – sent when needed i.e. to chase up payment, from solicitors etc

These are now considered in more detail.

1.3 Visits to trade receivables

Visits to trade receivables are helpful in assessing their ability to pay and secondly in sorting out any administrative problems. **Establishing good relations** with key personnel is always helpful in ensuring positive action and it clears the way for easier communication if problems or uncertainties arise.

However, these visits need **careful planning** to bring constructive attention to queried invoices and a follow-up visit may be necessary to resolve the problems. Visiting may be the only practical way of resolving queries on an account with hundreds of entries as long involved letters or telephone calls are too cumbersome to sort out a large problem. If the customer refuses to co-operate and does nothing to investigate problems, then the whole process can be very frustrating and the credit controller will need to employ much tact and diplomacy to make the visit worthwhile.

It is therefore advisable to do the following:

- **plan** the meeting by making an appointment to see someone in authority

- **prepare** the facts of the case carefully prior to the meeting, possibly by summarising the last six months' transactions and taking back-up schedules of the details

- make the most of the visit to get a general impression of the state of the factory, stock levels and staff attitudes

- **ascertain** why the account has become overdue and try to identify what steps the client is taking to avoid a repetition of the problems

- conduct the meeting **firmly and politely** whilst remaining responsive to problems and queries.

1.4 Telephone calls

Telephone calls are a **quick way** of making personal contact and of obtaining an immediate response. It is also a much quicker method than visiting customers; however, to be effective, the same approach needs to be adopted:

- **planning** and **preparation**
- contacting the **right person** with sufficient authority to act
- adopting the **right tone** to persuade the customer to pay
- concluding the call with an **agreed plan**.

Clients may employ delaying tactics, such as asking for copy invoices, which must be supplied promptly, but the caller must be receptive to signs of possible problems, e.g.:

- the customer says he is unable to pay or promises to send part-payment
- payments become later and later each month
- promises are persistently broken
- contra claims are made
- agreed points/plans are ignored and promises are broken.

In these cases, it is often advisable for the credit manager to take control and try to resolve the situation, for it may require legal action to obtain payment.

1.5 Collection letters

Collection letters are a quick and relatively easy way of contacting overdue trade receivables.

Each letter must convey the salient points, namely that:

- the trade receivable is late in paying
- the trade receivable is in breach of his credit terms
- payment is therefore due immediately.

A final reminder may be sent out if there is no response to the first. There is often little point in pursuing the trade receivable with many letters and sometimes a threat of legal action will result in prompt payment.

If further action is threatened, then the company must be prepared to carry out the threat whether it be to instruct solicitors, put the account out for collection or stop supplies. There are various letters that a credit controller may need to send out. These are described in the following sections.

1.6 First reminder letter

The first reminder letter is designed to **point out the facts**, the amount outstanding and as a reminder or encouragement to pay the amount due very soon. As with all letters to customers, it must be courteous and succinct as well as firm.

The first reminder letter will be sent out when the debts are a certain amount overdue. The timescale of the reminder letter will depend upon company policy towards debt collection but might be sent out 7 days after a debt becomes overdue. Therefore, if an invoice is sent to a customer with 30-day credit terms then the first reminder letter will be sent out 37 days after the invoice was sent out.

The first reminder letter will normally be sent to the person with day-to-day responsibility for payment of creditors rather than more senior management.

An example of a first reminder letter is given below:

HOWARD LTD
Dene Court
Hereford
HF3 9RT

6 April 20X4
Accounts Payable Manager
Westrope Ltd
Account no: **021547**

Dear Sir

Further to our invoices detailed below, I do not appear to have received payment. I trust that this is an oversight and that you will arrange for immediate payment to be made. If you are withholding payment for any reason, please contact me urgently and I will be pleased to assist you.

Invoice no	Terms	Due date	Amount £

If you have already made payment please advise me and accept my apology for having troubled you.

Yours faithfully

Janet Bernard
Credit Control Manager

1.7 Final reminder letter

If there is no response from the initial reminder letter then there will tend to be little point in sending a second reminder letter. However, in some instances a telephone call at this stage is useful to clear up any misunderstanding and to assess whether further action is required.

The options for a company are to put the debt into the hands of a debt collector, to take the company to court for payment or to suspend any further sales to the company until payment is received. Whatever action the company decides to take, a final reminder letter must be sent to the customer detailing this action if payment is not received.

At this stage, the final reminder letter will normally be sent to a senior member of the management team such as the chief accountant or finance director.

An example of each type of final reminder letter is given below.

1.8 Debt collectors

HOWARD LTD
Dene Court
Hereford
HF3 9RT

12 April 20X4
Finance Director
Westrope Ltd
Account no: **021547**

Dear Sir

Further to our invoices detailed below and the reminder letter dated 6 April 20X4, I do not appear to have received payment. If you are withholding payment for any reason, please contact me urgently and I will be pleased to assist you.

Invoice no	Terms	Due date	Amount £

I regret that unless payment is received within the next seven days I will have no alternative but to put the collection of the amounts due into the hands of a third party. If you have already made the payment please advise me and accept my apology for having troubled you.

Yours faithfully

Janet Bernard
Credit Control Manager

1.9 Legal action

HOWARD LTD
Dene Court
Hereford
HF3 9RT

12 April 20X4
Finance Director
Westrope Ltd
Account no: **021547**
Total amount outstanding: **£2,279.50**

Dear Sir

Despite the previous reminders and telephone calls we have still not received your payment in settlement of the above account total. You have promised payment on a number of occasions but no payment has been received to date.

We regret that due to the above we have no alternative but to consider the Small Claim procedure in the County Court in order to recover the sum outstanding. Prior to us taking such action we would however wish to give you one final opportunity to make payment. We will therefore delay submission of the claim to the County Court for a period of seven days from the date of this letter in the hope that the account is settled. We will not enter into further correspondence regarding this matter other than through the County Court.

Please note that if we are forced to take legal action you may become liable for the costs of such action which, if successful, may affect your future credit rating.

Yours faithfully

Janet Bernard
Credit Control Manager

1.10 Stopping sales

HOWARD LTD
Dene Court
Hereford
HF3 9RT

Date: 12 April 20X4
Finance Director
Westrope Ltd
Account no: **021547**

Dear Sir

Further to our invoices detailed below, I do not appear to have received payment. I trust that this is an oversight and that you will arrange for immediate payment to be made. If you are withholding payment for any reason, please contact me urgently and I will be pleased to assist you.

Invoice no	Terms	Due date	Amount £

I regret that unless payment is received within the next seven days I will have no alternative but to stop any further sales on credit to you until the amount owing is cleared in full. If you have made payment please advise me and accept my apology for having troubled you.

Yours faithfully

Janet Bernard
Credit Control Manager

1.11 Courtesy and tact

Throughout all the communications with customers, it is important to remember that the **aim is to persuade them to pay their bill**. A firm approach is needed in all dealings to ensure this message is understood. Credit controllers should act with authority as late payment is in breach of the credit terms.

It is important that people with good interpersonal skills communicate with the customer to avoid unnecessary acrimony.

It is also important that pursuit of the customer is discreet and confidential. Broadcasting to the business community that a certain business is not paying its bills can have severe effects on that business, and may even result in libel writs.

2 Refusal of credit

2.1 Introduction

In many cases, once the credit manager has carried out checks on a new potential customer such as bank references, trade references, credit agency reports and analysis of financial statements, then a decision will be made to grant the customer credit and the terms of payment will be communicated to the new customer. However, in some cases, the credit manager may decide that it is not possible to trade with a new potential customer on credit terms.

2.2 Possible reasons for refusal of credit

The decision to refuse to grant credit to a new customer is a big decision for the credit manager as the business will not wish to lose this potential customer's business, but the credit manager will have taken a view that the risk of non-payment from the customer is too high for credit terms to be granted.

Refusal of credit does not necessarily mean that the potential customer's business is bad or is likely not to survive, it simply means that on the evidence available to the credit manager the risk of non-payment is too high for the company to take the risk.

There are a variety of reasons why a credit manager may decide against granting of credit which include the following:

- a non-committal or poor bank reference

- poor trade references

- concerns about the validity of any trade references submitted

- adverse press comment about the potential customer

- poor credit agency report

- indications of business weakness from analysis of the financial statements

- lack of historical financial statements due to being a recently started company.

The credit manager will consider all of the evidence available about a potential customer and the reason for the refusal of credit may be due to a single factor noted above or a combination of factors.

2.3   Communication of refusal of credit

If credit is not to be granted to a potential customer then this must be communicated to the customer in a **tactful and diplomatic manner**. The **reasons** for the refusal of credit must be politely explained and any **future actions** required from the potential customer should also be made quite clear. The credit manager, whilst not wishing to grant credit to the customer at the current time, equally does not necessarily want to lose the potential business of this customer.

2.4   Trading on cash terms

In almost all cases where credit is to be refused to a potential customer, the company should make it quite clear that they would be happy to **trade with the customer on cash terms**. This may be acceptable to the customer, although not desirable, and the business will not be lost.

2.5   Future re-assessment of creditworthiness

In some cases, although the granting of credit to the new customer has been refused now, it may be that the credit manager wishes to encourage the customer to **apply for credit terms in the future**. For example, with a newly formed company there may be little external information on which the credit manager can rely at the current time but if financial statements and references can be provided in the future then the decision as to whether or not to trade on credit terms in future can be re-assessed.

2.6   Telephone or letter?

In most cases it may be most appropriate to communicate the reasons for the **refusal of credit initially in a letter**. However, in such a letter the credit manager may suggest that a further telephone call might be appropriate in order to discuss the matter and any future actions that may be necessary.

Example

You are the credit manager for Howard Ltd and your name is Belinda Sean. You have recently been assessing requests for credit from three potential new customers.

Kenwick Partners – they have requested to purchase goods from you, would like a £5,000 credit limit and 60 days' credit. You asked for trade references and bank references and financial statements for the last three years. They have provided you with a bank reference which states that 'the partnership appears to be well constituted but we cannot necessarily speak for your figures due to the length of time that the partnership has been in operation'. They have also provided one trade reference which is satisfactory from a company which allows Kenwick £2,000 of credit on 30-day terms. However, the partnership has only been in operation for nine months and therefore they have not been able to provide you with any financial statements.

Fisher Ltd – this company has requested credit limit of £5,000 from your company and 30 days' credit. Two trade references have been provided (but no bank reference),along with the last set of published financial statements which include the previous years' comparative figures. The trade references appeared satisfactory although one is from Barnaby & Sons and it has been noted that the managing director of Fisher Ltd is Mr R Barnaby.

Analysis of the financial statements has indicated a decrease in profitability during the last year, a high level of gearing and low liquidity ratios.

Jacob Enterprises Ltd - this company is requesting 30 days of credit and a credit limit of £4,000. They have provided their balance sheet at their yearend which was four months ago and the profit and loss account for the year to that date. The financial statements indicate fairly low levels of profitability but there is nothing to compare the figures to. The bank reference is satisfactory but of the two trade references one has only been trading with Jacob Enterprises for two months.

You are to draft suitable letters to each potential customer.

Solution

HOWARD LTD
Dene Court
Dene Park
Hereford
HF3 9RT

Finance Director
Kenwick Partners
Kenwick House
Green Land
Watnall

Dear Sir

Re: Request for credit facilities

Thank you for your enquiry regarding the provision of credit facilities by us for £5,000 of credit on 60 day terms. We have taken up your trade and bank references which you kindly sent details of.

We have some concerns about offering credit at this early stage of your business as there are, as yet, no financial statements for your business that we can examine. Therefore, at this stage I am unable to confirm whether we can provide you with credit facilities.

We would of course be delighted to trade with you on cash terms until we have had an opportunity to examine your first year's trading figures. Therefore, please send us a copy of your first year financial statements when they are available and in the meantime contact us if you would like to start trading on a cash basis.

Thank you for your interest in our company.

Yours faithfully

Belinda Sean,

Belinda Sean
Credit Manager

HOWARD LTD
Dene Court
Dene Park
Hereford
HF3 9RT

Finance Director
Fisher Ltd
Farm Road Industrial Park
Fordtown

Dear Sir

Re: Request for credit facilities

Thank you for your enquiry regarding the provision of credit facilities by us for £5,000 of credit on 30 day terms. We have taken up your trade references and examined your latest set of financial statements.

We are unfortunately concerned about your levels of profitability in the most recent year and also have some concerns about one of the trade references from Barnaby & Sons.

On balance we are not in a position to grant your request for trade credit at the current time, although we would of course be delighted to trade with you on a cash basis. If you do not wish to trade on this basis and would like to enquire about credit terms in the future then we would be delighted to examine your current year's financial statements when they are available.

Thank you for your interest in our company.

Yours faithfully

Belinda Sean

Belinda Sean
Credit Manager

HOWARD LTD
Dene Court
Dene Park
Hereford
HF3 9RT

Finance Director
Jacob Enterprises Ltd
White Hill
Blacktown

Dear Sir

Re: Request for credit facilities

Thank you for your enquiry regarding the provision of credit facilities by us for £4,000 of credit on 30 day terms. We have taken up your trade references and examined your latest set of financial statements.

We have some concerns about your level of profitability and would like the opportunity to examine your balance sheets and profit and loss accounts for the two previous years. As one of your trade references has only been trading with you for two months, we would request details of a further supplier that we could contact for a trade reference.

At this stage I am unable to confirm whether we can provide you with a credit facility but will reconsider the situation when we receive your financial statements and additional trade reference.

Thank you for your interest in our company and in the meantime we would of course be delighted to trade with you on a cash terms basis.

Yours faithfully

Belinda Sean,

Belinda Sean
Credit Manager

Activity 1

You are the credit manager for Style Ltd and your name is Henry H Oover. You have recently been assessing requests for credit from potential new customers.

NY Partners have requested to purchase goods from you, would like a £4,000 credit limit and 60 days' credit. You asked for trade references and bank references and financial statements for the last three years. They have provided you with a bank reference which states that 'the partnership appears to be well constituted but we cannot necessarily speak for your figures due to the length of time that the partnership has been in operation'. They have also provided one trade reference which is satisfactory from a company which allows NY Partners £2,000 of credit on 30-day terms. However, the partnership has only been in operation for nine months and therefore they have not been able to provide you with any financial statements.

You are to draft a suitable letter to this potential customer.

2.7 Trial period for credit

In some cases there may be some concerns about the information available about a potential new customer, but perhaps not enough of a concern to refuse to grant credit. In such circumstances it might be appropriate to **grant a degree of credit to the customer on a trial basis** with review of the situation at some point in the future.

For example, if a potential customer's trade references show that in one case although the customer has been given 30 days of credit they generally take 60 days to pay, then your company may offer them a fairly low credit limit on 30-day terms and monitor the situation for, say, six months when the situation will be re-assessed.

 Example

You are again the credit manager for Howard Ltd and your name is Belinda Sean. You have been assessing the financial statements for Reed & Sons who have requested £6,000 of credit on 60-day terms. You also have received a satisfactory bank reference and trade references.

Your analysis of the 20X3 and 20X2 financial statements show the following picture:

	20X3	20X2
Gross profit margin	28%	30%
Net profit margin	4%	3%
Interest cover	1.5 times	0.9 times
Current ratio	1.3 times	0.8 times

You are to draft a suitable letter to Reed & Sons dealing with their request for credit facilities.

Solution

HOWARD LTD
Dene Court
Dene Park
Hereford
HF3 9RT

Finance Director
Reed & Sons
Ghyll Farm Development
Steel Cross

Dear Sir

Re: Request for credit facilities

Thank you for your enquiry regarding the provision of credit facilities by us for £6,000 of credit on 60 day terms. We have taken up your bank and trade references and examined your latest set of financial statements.

Although your references are satisfactory, we have some concerns about your profitability and liquidity. Clearly, your overall profitability and liquidity position have improved since 20X2 but their levels are still lower than we would normally accept in order to grant a credit facility.

However, due to your bank and trade references, we would be happy to offer you a credit facility for six months at the end of which period the movement on your account would be reviewed and the position re-assessed. The credit limit that we could offer you would initially be £2,000 and the payment terms would be strictly 30 days from the invoice date.

Thank you for your interest in our company and we look forward to trading with you on the basis set out above.

Yours sincerely

Belinda Sean

Belinda Sean
Credit Manager

3 Payment methods

3.1 Introduction

A variety of payment methods are available in the UK for credit customers. The choice between them depends upon:

(a) the user (business or personal)

(b) the frequency of the payment (regular or one-off)

(c) convenience, and

(d) cost.

3.2 Cash

Some customers still pay by cash. Although this is an instantaneous payment, with no delays attached to drawing the money, it involves cumbersome visits to the bank to deposit the money and it is sometimes hard to allocate the money to a specific invoice in the accounts.

3.3 Cheque

Many customers still pay by cheques (or banker's drafts for very high value transactions) which pass through a clearing system to transfer the money from the customer's to the supplier's bank account. Cheques take three days to clear through the system.

3.4 Cheque crossings

 Definition

A cheque crossing is two vertical lines on the face of a cheque with or without some additional words.

Cheques can have a number of different types of crossing and you need to be aware of the meaning of these.

A general crossing is two vertical lines on the face of the cheque. This crossing instructs the paying bank to make payment only to another bank.

A special crossing is where the name of the collecting bank is written across the cheque. The cheque can then only be paid to the bank stated.

When 'not negotiable' is written between the lines of the crossing this means that in a case of fraud the person given the cheque has no better rights to it than the person who gave it to them. Therefore if A steals a cheque and gives it to B in payment for goods, if the cheque has a not negotiable crossing then B has no right to the cheque.

If 'account payee' is written across the cheque crossing this is an instruction to the collecting bank that the cheque must only be paid into the bank account of the original payee.

Most pre-printed cheques these days have the account payee crossing.

3.5 Dates on cheques

If cheques are received as payment from trade receivables then it is important that the date is checked.

If the cheque is dated **more than six months ago** then the banks will view it as a **stale cheque** and will return it unpaid.

If the cheque is post-dated, i.e. dated after today's date, then technically it cannot be paid into the bank until the date shown on the cheque.

3.6 Stopped cheque

A customer can stop payment of a cheque after it has been written and sent out by instructing its bank in writing not to pay the cheque unless by using the related cheque guarantee card the bank is committed to honour the cheque.

3.7 Cheque guarantee card

If a cheque guarantee card is used when payment is made then the bank is **committed to pay the cheque** even if this results in an unauthorised overdraft.

3.8 High value payments

 Definition

The Clearing House Automated Payments System (CHAPS) is an electronic, inter-bank, on-line, real-time credit clearing system for guaranteed same-day value sterling payments.

It is a system which has grown rapidly because of its nationwide electronic access capability, its ability to handle large volumes and its relatively low operating costs. The system allows for payments to be transmitted (on a real-time basis) from one bank branch to another. Settlement is effected electronically after the cut-off time each day across settlement members' accounts at the Bank of England. Such transactions are irrevocable and unconditional from the time they enter the system and consequently high levels of security are maintained.

3.9 Bulk electronic clearing

Most items of low value and of a repetitive nature (wages, other credit transfers, direct debits) are dealt with through the **BACS system**. Settlements occur after three days and are effected by payment instructions submitted via magnetic media or by a direct telecommunications link to the BACS centre. There the items are sorted and instructions sent out to clearing banks' and building societies' computer centres. The cost of BACS is significantly less than other methods.

3.10 Direct debit

A direct debit allows the supplier to obtain payment direct from the customer's bank on presentation either of manually prepared direct debit vouchers or a computer magnetic tape. It is a system which deals equally well with **regular or irregular amounts** but, although it offers considerable administrative savings, the supplier may find that dealing with dishonoured payments is very time-consuming and considerable effort is required to set up direct debit payments.

3.11 Credit cards

A customer effectively borrows money from a credit card company to pay the supplier; the supplier pays a fee (up to 4% of the transaction value) to operate the system.

3.12 Debit cards

Here, the customer allows the supplier to transfer money directly from his account to the supplier's account. It is an alternative to paying by cash or writing a cheque and is becoming increasingly popular.

4 Debt collection procedures

4.1 Introduction

The collection of cash starts by **sending invoices and statements**. It is helpful to file a **goods received note** in the credit management system as this helps credit controllers to substantiate claims of delivery. These notes must be diligently filed, having been signed by the recipient, dated and pre-numbered, and matched with invoices.

Many customers do not pay their invoices promptly and a **polite reminder** is often needed. Other customers require more than a gentle reminder and it may be necessary to take legal action to obtain payment from certain buyers.

It is important to have a **planned approach** to non-payment problems to ensure that the company's cash flow is not severely affected. The following sequence of events should be effective.

(1)   The problem must be identified, in terms of the value of unpaid accounts, the number and age.

(2)   This problem must then be broken down into manageable units and individuals given responsibility to collect in the debts from each unit.

(3)   A plan of action must be agreed. This may include visiting, phoning, faxing, emailing, sending reminders and other suitable techniques to encourage payment.

(4)   The results of these actions must be monitored and reported to managers who can take more serious steps of a legal nature if necessary.

4.2   The action plan for debt collection

A possible timescale might be as follows:

	Date
Customer places order	1 January
↓	
Credit limit is checked	2/3 January
↓	
Delivery note raised and goods are delivered	8 January
↓	
Invoiced raised	15 January
↓	
Statement of all invoices	31 January
↓	
Follow up procedures	1-14 February
↓	
Cash received from customer	15 February

The length of follow-up period will depend on whether the customer has merely overlooked payment or is trying to extend credit terms further.

In most cases **with good credit control procedures monies will be received** from credit customers sometimes after encouragement such as reminder letters or telephone calls. However there will no doubt be some cases in which either the debt is never collected and has to be written off or the business has to resort to legal procedures to obtain payment. Before we consider these matters there are other methods that a business can use to minimise the possibility of either of these two occurrences.

5 Monitoring debt collection

5.1 Introduction

The credit manager should closely monitor the collection of debts. Since this is of such fundamental importance to the cash flow, it is a regular if not daily task. It is important for all the departments in the company to pool their collective knowledge.

The credit manager needs to warn the sales department of:

(a) customers who are building up a significant outstanding account

(b) customers who have not paid for a long period of time

(c) customers whose cheques have been dishonoured by their bank.

Liaison between the two should warn the sales department that the customer may be having problems and be wary on the next visit of any further signs of this.

5.2 Analysis of the aged trade receivables listing

The regular review of the aged trade receivable analysis should highlight the following potential problems:

- credit limit exceeded
- slow payers
- recent debts cleared but older outstanding amount
- old amounts outstanding and no current trading.

Each of these will be considered in turn.

5.3 Credit limited exceeded

If a customer's account balance shows that their credit limit has been exceeded then this must be investigated.

This is sometimes due to a **lack of communication** between the sales department and the sales ledger department. However, before a new sale on credit is agreed with a credit customer, it should be standard practice to ensure that this new sale will not mean that the customer has exceeded the agreed credit limit.

If a customer is highlighted in the aged trade receivable listing as having exceeded their credit limit then normally the customer should be told that **no further sales** will be made to them until at least some of the outstanding balances have been repaid. However, in some circumstances, liaison between the sales ledger and the sales department may result in an **increase in the customer's credit limit** if they have a good payment record and are simply increasing their trade with our company rather than just delaying payment of the amounts due.

5.4 Slow payers

Some businesses can be identified from the aged trade receivable listing as being slow payers as they always have amounts **outstanding for, say, 31 to 60 days and 61 to 90 days as well as current amounts**. In these cases consideration should be given to methods of encouraging the customer to pay earlier. This could be in the form of a letter from the finance director or perhaps more successfully the offer of a settlement discount for earlier payment.

5.5 Recent debts cleared but older outstanding amount

If a customer is generally a regular payer and the most recent debts have been cleared but there is still an outstanding older amount then this will normally indicate either a **query over the amount outstanding** or a problem with the recording of invoices, credit notes or payments received.

If there appears to be no communication with the trade receivable about a queried invoice that would account for the old debt outstanding then the invoice postings, credit note postings and payments received from that trade receivable should be checked to ensure that there have been no errors which have resulted in the recording of this outstanding amount. If there appear to be no errors then the trade receivable should be contacted in order to find out what the problem is concerning payment of this particular amount.

5.6 Old amounts outstanding and no current trading

This is probably the most concerning situation for a credit manager. In this case it would appear that the **trade receivable is no longer buying from us** but still owes us money from previous purchases. In this case the trade receivable should be contacted immediately and payment sought. If no contact can be made with the trade receivable or there is a genuine problem with payment, such as bankruptcy or liquidation, consideration should be given to writing off the debt as bad.

Specific provision for doubtful debts

As soon as there is a problem with a trade receivable which indicates he may be unable to pay a debt, it is **prudent to provide against the debt**. A specific provision can be set up for debts and a list is compiled of:

(a)   invoices disputed

(b)   invoices with warranty claims

(c)   part-payment invoices

(d)   old invoices

(e)   suspense account items,

and the total figure forms part of the specific provision and is written off against the year's profit.

Assessing bad debts

As the person dealing with the accounts of trade receivables and analysing the aged trade receivable analysis, you are in a position to be able to assess potential bad debts. You should ensure that when doing this you use all available information. This might include the following:

- evidence of long outstanding debts from the aged debt analysis

- a one-off outstanding debt when more recent debts have been cleared

- correspondence with trade receivables

- outstanding older debts and no current business with the customer

- press comment

- information from the sales team.

Communicating potential bad debts

If you believe that a debt is bad or perhaps doubtful then it will normally not be your decision to actually write the debt off or provide against it. This will normally be the decision of a more senior person in the accounting function. Therefore, if you have information about potential bad or doubtful debts then all of this information should be communicated clearly to the relevant person within the accounting function.

Incidence of bad debts

It can be argued that a high level of bad debts in an organisation is an indicator of poor credit control, although there could obviously be other reasons such as the general economic climate. A high level of bad debts could be an indication of:

- sales being made to high risk customers

- poor assessment of creditworthiness

- lack of useful information for checking on creditworthiness

- weak sales ledger accounting

- poor follow up procedures for outstanding debts.

Example

Wood Limited

Trade receivables' age analysis at 31.12.X1

Account no	Name	Credit limit	Total	Up to 30 days	31-60 days	61-90 days	Over 90 days
		£	£	£	£	£	£
A001	ABC Limited	10,000	9,580	9,500	–	80	–
A002	DEF Limited	20,000	400	400	–	–	–
A003	GHI Limited	15,000	14,000	10,000	3,000	1,000	–
A004	JKL Limited	2,500	2,500	–	–	2,000	500
A005	MNO Limited	3,500	4,000	1,500	2,500	–	–
.	.	.	.	.	.	.	.
.	.	.	.	.	.	.	.
Total			30,480	21,400	5,500	3,080	500
%			100	70.2	18.0	10.2	1.6

Solution

Taking each trade receivable in turn we will consider what information the aged debt analysis has provided and what further action might be taken.

ABC Ltd   The vast majority of this debt is current therefore there may be some dispute over the £80 over 60 days old which should be investigated.

DEF Ltd   There would appear to be no problems with this account.

GHI Ltd   This would appear to be a slow payer and encouragement should be given to pay the older debts.

JKL Ltd   This trade receivable is a concern. There has been no trading with this customer in the last two months and their full credit limit has been used and is still outstanding after 61 and 90 days.

MNO Ltd This trade receivable has been allowed to exceed the credit limit set by £500. The reason for this should be investigated and either supplies should be stopped until some of the outstanding balance has been cleared or the credit limit should be reassessed.

The percentage of each ageing of total trade receivables is also useful information for the credit manager as any increase in the older trade receivables percentage would be a cause for concern.

 Activity 2

Jones Limited has sold goods on credit to Smith Plc. The following information is available.

(i)   Aged trade receivable analysis

(ii)   Copies of outstanding invoices

(iii) Copies of trade references

(iv) Copies of contractual documents

(v)   Copies of bank references

Which of the above will be needed to aid collection of the debts from Smith Plc?

A   All items

B   (i), (ii) and (iii) only

C ✓ (i), (ii) and (iv) only   ✓

D   (iii) and (v) only

5.7   Updating the aged trade receivable analysis

The aged trade receivable analysis can be prepared by updating the previous analysis for any invoices issued in the period and any cash received in the period. The monthly balance, if still remaining unpaid, must then move into the column representing one month further outstanding. For example, if an invoice in the 'up to 30 days' column is not paid in the following month then it moves into the '31 to 60 days' column.

Example

Given below is an extract from the aged trade receivable analysis for a company at 30 April 20X4

Account	Name	Credit limit £	Total £	Up to 30 days £	31–60 days £	61 – 90 days £	> 90 days £
0001	Ace Partners	6,000	4,800	2,100 inv 0257	1,700 inv 0244	1,000 inv 0211	
0002	Aflek Ltd	10,000	8,850	4,550 inv 0259	4,000 inv 0247		300 inv 0196
0003	Amber Ltd	5,000	2,400	2,400 inv 0252			

During the month of May 20X4 the following transactions took place with these trade receivables:

Ace Partners   Invoice 0269 issued for £1,800
Paid invoice   0211
Aflek Ltd   Invoice 0266 issued for £1,300
                Paid half of invoice 0247
Amber Ltd   Invoice 0273 issued for £2,200

Update the aged trade receivable analysis to reflect the transactions in May 20X4.

Solution

Account	Name	Credit limit £	Total £	Up to 30 days £	31–60 days £	61 – 90 days £	> 90 days £
0001	Ace Partners	6,000	5,600	1,800 inv 0269	2,100 Inv 0257	1,700 Inv 0244	
0002	Aflek Ltd	10,000	8,150	1,300 inv 0266	4,550 Inv 0259	2,000 Inv 0247	300 Inv 0196
0003	Amber Ltd	5,000	4,600	2,200 inv 0273	2,400 Inv 0252		

5.8 Debt collection policy

Each company will have its own version of the debt collect policy below is an example (as seen in chapter 2):

Debt collection process

- Invoices to be despatched on day of issue, (day of issue to be no more than 2 days after date of delivery).
- Statements to be despatched in the second week of the month.
- Aged trade receivable analysis to be produced and reviewed on a weekly basis.

- Reminder letter to be sent once an account is overdue.

- Telephone chaser for accounts 15 days overdue.

- Customer on stop list if no payment is received within 5 days of the telephone chaser. Computerised sales order processing system updated and automatic email sent to the customer contact and the account manager (sales person).

- Letter threatening legal action if payment not received within 30 days of the first letter

- Legal proceedings / debt collection agency instructed subject to the approval of the Finance Director.

- Prepare a report suggesting an appropriate provision for bad or doubtful debts.

If at any stage in the process the customer is declared insolvent or bankrupt then contact the insolvency practitioner in order to register the debt and notify the financial accountant so that the VAT can be reclaimed.

Activity 3

Put the following in a sensible order for a debt collection policy

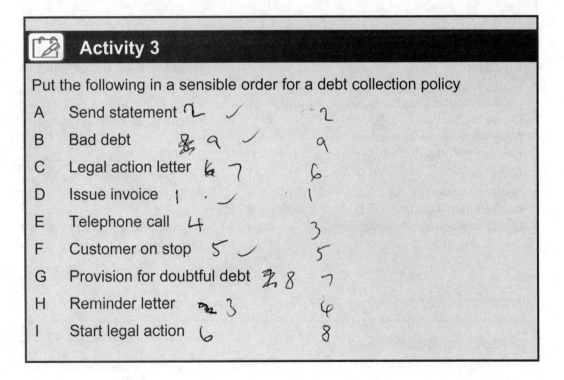

A	Send statement	2		2
B	Bad debt	9		9
C	Legal action letter	7		6
D	Issue invoice	1		1
E	Telephone call	4		3
F	Customer on stop	5		5
G	Provision for doubtful debt	8		7
H	Reminder letter	3		4
I	Start legal action	6		8

Activity 4

You are working in Wilson Limited's credit control section. The Sales Manager has asked for your views on the credit status of four organisations to whom Wilson Limited supplies goods. Using the extracts from the aged analysis of trade receivables given below, analyse these four accounts and write a memorandum to the Sales Manager.

Your memorandum should:

- provide an opinion of the creditworthiness of the customer and the status of the account

- suggest how the account should be managed in future.

Customer name and address	Current month	Total due	Up to 30 days	Up to 60 days	Up to 90 days	Over 90 days
	£	£	£	£	£	£
Megacorp plc						
Oakham, Rutland	10,000	72,540	11,250	12,250	15,500	23,540
Credit limit	85,000		Terms of sale: 60 days net			
Goodfellows Cycles						
Limited, Manchester	9,500	24,000	9,500			5,000
Credit limit	50,000		Terms of sale: 30 days net			
Hooper-bikes						
Limited, Sheffield	5,000	26,750	6,250	4,875	5,275	5,350
Credit limit	25,000		Terms of sale: 60 days net			
Dynamo Cycles						
Limited, Nottingham	4,500	7,250	2,750			
Credit limit	7,500		Terms of sale: 30 days net			

MEMORANDUM

To: Sales Manager

Date: XX-XX-XX

From: Credit controller

Subject: Credit status of organisations

---

6 Factoring

6.1 Factoring arrangements

🔍 Definition

Factoring involves the use of a factoring company to provide sales ledger services, finance and in some cases protection against bad debts in return for a fee.

A company may wish to farm out the collection of its debts through a factoring arrangement. This relieves the company of the burden of maintaining a detailed credit control system.

A factoring arrangement can be taken out with a factoring company (the 'factor'). Factoring companies are generally controlled by the clearing banks which gives considerable credence to the industry.

6.2 Options available

The factoring arrangement usually allows for the following.

(a) **Administration of the sales ledger and credit control functions**. The factor takes over all operations on the credit side from credit approval to collecting the cash. This facility only leaves the client the work of raising invoices and clearing disputes, as the factoring company effectively runs the sales ledger. The customer has little need for a sophisticated computer system; the cost of such a scheme is between 0.75% and 3% of turnover.

(b) **Finance**. If the company requires cash immediately, the factoring company may provide up to 85% of the value of the debt immediately. This is effectively a cash advance and usually costs slightly more than bank borrowing rates. However, the payment is certain and allows for a determined cash flow.

(c) **Credit protection**. This can be provided by the factor to cover against bad debts. If the factoring agreement is 'without recourse' then the factor bears the risk of any trade receivables that do not pay. If the agreement is 'with recourse' then the customer will have to repay to the factor any monies advanced for the debt that is bad.

6.3 Advantages of debt factoring

Factoring is particularly useful in the early stages of development when a company is sufficiently large to need to devote attention to trade receivables but not yet large enough to warrant employing a full-time credit manager.

The advantages of debt factoring are as follows.

- The company need **no longer incur the costs** of employing its own debt collection staff.

- Because the factor can act for several companies concurrently, the client will benefit from the **economies of scale** of such an organisation and the factor's fees are reduced.

- The **cash flow advantages** that ensue from a regular predetermined cash inflow should reduce the company's financing charges thereby improving liquidity.

One of the main disadvantages of factoring is that control of trade receivables is surrendered to the factor which may **displease customers** or give the **impression of liquidity problems** in the company.

7 Invoice discounting

7.1 Invoice discounting

Invoice discounting is the purchase of invoices from a company, but, unlike debt factoring, the **invoice discounter does not take over control of debt collection**. The invoice discounter solely supplies an advance of cash.

The main advantage of this system is that **trade receivables remain unaware** of the arrangement.

From the invoice discounter's point of view, this method of advancing money on debts is **more risky than debt factoring**, for the discounter does not control debt collection and relies on the company to collect the debt for them. Therefore such a service may only be available to companies with reliable, well established collection procedures.

 Activity 5

Invoice discounting is:

A   A reduced price for goods

B   A reduced price for early payment

C ✓ A finance house lending money against invoices issued

D   A judgement by court

8 Debt insurance

8.1 Debt insurance

Debt insurance is a method of **guarding against unexpected failures**. Credit management is still required but it is a way of safeguarding one's cash flow. It may be particularly useful when a company deals with one or two major customers and is therefore dependent upon them.

Debt insurance or **credit insurance** is obtained through a broker who establishes terms and an agreement between the insured and the underwriter. The broker receives a commission for his work and, if he negotiates the policy well, will be able to renew it in the following year.

The types of cover available fall into four main categories:

(a) whole turnover

(b) datum line

(c) catastrophe

(d) specific account

allowing the insured to insure different types of debts.

8.2 Selecting the correct policy

Each company will have its own system of credit control and its own pattern of sales/trade receivables. Entire turnover policies are available to cover all possible bad debts, usually with a de minimis limit, but these are often very expensive. A more specific policy can be taken out, such as a datum line policy, which covers customers whose indebtedness exceeds an agreed amount.

Alternatively, a policy-holder may decide to exclude certain large customers in whom he has full confidence and so the policy becomes quite specific in its nature with only certain individual accounts insured.

8.3 Terms of the policy

Most policies insure between 75% and 90% of agreed sales. The premium is negotiable between the parties.

A credit limit will need to be agreed for each customer. This is sometimes a difficult part to negotiate as the insured may well require a higher level of credit to cover the expected trade with the customer than the underwriter is prepared to accept. Trading above the agreed limit may invalidate the policy; but having to restrict sales to the customer may lose goodwill. A good relationship with the underwriter may help to solve this problem.

8.4 Pre-shipment insurance

Pre-shipment insurance is available to cover work-in-progress losses or losses of finished goods. It offers protection for orders cancelled at the last minute where there is no alternative buyer and only scrap value is obtainable.

8.5 Catastrophe policies

The main features of catastrophe policies are as follows:

(a) the insured agrees to bear the first £1,000, say, of the loss due to the catastrophe

(b) above this aggregate limit the cover will reimburse a specified percentage of the loss

(c) this policy is not normally suitable for small companies.

Credit insurance is a means of **protecting against bad debts**; however, it is usually a **costly** way of obtaining security and many companies may decide to bear the cost of bad debts themselves when they are confident that this is less expensive than the insurance premium.

 Activity 6

Credit insurance enables a company to claim for:

A ✓ debts that a customer has not paid

B missed mortgage payments

C missed loan payments

D overdue payments to creditors

9 Stopping supplies

9.1 Stopping supplies

Stopping supplies is one way of **preventing a problem escalating** with an overdue trade receivable. The credit manager must protect the company's investment and minimise the chance of a bad debt.

There are various reasons for non-payment of debts: the customer may be unable to pay, be inefficient, or be dissatisfied.

- If the customer is unable to pay the supplier must safeguard his own position and ceasing to supply will prevent the debt increasing; however, the customer may claim he is able to trade out of the problem for which purpose he needs continuing supplies. The supplier needs to be quite convinced of this before releasing more goods.

- Inefficiencies may be quickly resolved by the prospect of a stoppage in supplies and this is often a useful jolt to rectify the position. If there is dissatisfaction over the supply of goods, however, stopping supplies is unlikely to resolve the problem.

- Customers who deliberately fail to pay need to be dropped from the sales ledger. Although there is often great reluctance to do this – particularly in small firms where there is a fear of losing business – it is the only answer.

10 Collection agencies

10.1 Collection agencies

A collection agency can be appointed to collect debts. Various types of agency exist but they can generally be split into three types:

(a) **trade associations** are usually non-profit making bodies who charge an annual membership fee and a percentage of the monies recovered

(b) **voucher agencies** sell books of collection vouchers to client companies who are entitled to complete a voucher for any outstanding debt and send it to the agency

(c) **commercial agencies** who usually work on a 'no-collection, no-charge' basis.

Collection agencies have the advantage of relieving the credit manager of the time-consuming work of chasing customers. A good agency will be specialised in tracing trade receivables who have disappeared, and will often have legal expertise. The charge is reasonable compared with the cost of employing another member of staff.

However, if the credit manager has a good efficient staff they may be able to do the work and so save the costs of an agency. Customers rarely respond well to outside agencies whose sole aim is to obtain payment of a debt and goodwill can easily be lost by such steps. However if a customer is regularly defaulting on payment then debt collection agencies can have more of a impact on said customer.

It is usually sensible to check that the agency:

(a) is of good standing in the locality

(b) is licensed for debt collection under the Consumer Credit Act 1974

(c) is financially sound

(d) uses an audited client trust account with its bank

(e) reports regularly to the company and returns payments promptly.

Activity 7

Debt collection agencies are used because:

A   They have extra powers to collect debts

B   The can stop other companies supplying goods to the trade receivable with the outstanding debt

C   They have the right to take goods from the trade receivable

D ✓ Customers take more notice of them and are therefore more likely to pay.

11 Summary

There are a variety of methods for collection of debts which may help businesses in different circumstances. Factoring arrangements can relieve a business of having to collect its own debts and can also be useful for cash flow purposes if funds are advanced and the debts are collected by the factor. Invoice discounting also allows money to be advanced to the business but still the business has the job of collecting their own debts. Debt insurance is a way of guarding against the non-payment of debts but is often a fairly expensive option. A collection agency can be used for collection of debts but this often has an adverse effect on the goodwill of the business. As a final resort a business can bring legal action to recover its debts, usually in the County Court or the High Court. If an individual is made bankrupt or a company goes into liquidation, then the unsecured creditors are some of the last to be paid and may well receive only a small amount of that which is owed to them or possibly none at all.

Answers to chapter activities

Activity 1

Dear Sir

Re: Request for credit facilities

Thank you for your enquiry regarding the provision of credit facilities by us for £4,000 of credit on 60 day terms. We have taken up your trade and bank references which you kindly sent details of.

We have some concerns about offering credit at this early stage of your business as there are, as yet, no financial statements for your business that we can examine. Therefore, at this stage I am unable to confirm whether we can provide you with credit facilities.

We would of course be delighted to trade with you on cash terms until we have had an opportunity to examine your first year's trading figures. Therefore, please send us a copy of your first year financial statements when they are available and in the meantime contact us if you would like to start trading on a cash basis.

Thank you for your interest in our company.

Yours faithfully

Activity 2

Answer C

Activity 3

Put the following in a sensible order for a debt collection policy

D   Issue invoice

A   Send statement

E   Telephone call

H   Reminder letter

F   Customer on stop

KAPLAN PUBLISHING

C	Legal action letter
G	Provision for doubtful debt
I	Start legal action
B	Bad debt

There are alternative that would also be considered sensible ie the reminder letter may be sent before the telephone call is made, the provision for doubtful debt may be provided earlier in the process.

 Activity 4

MEMORANDUM

To: Sales Manager

Date: XX-XX-XX

From: Credit controller

Subject: Credit status of organisations

Megacorp plc

Megacorp enjoys a high credit limit from our company. However the company is a poor payer and abuses the 60 days net terms of sale. Ways in which the account might be managed in the future include:

- The use of discounts for early payment or cash sale.

- Develop a better relationship with the customer to ensure prompt payment.

- Consider ways of providing a better service to Megacorp to facilitate prompt payment.

Goodfellows Cycles Limited

Goodfellows enjoys a relatively high level of credit from our company, of which it does not make excessive use. It is a prompt payer, with the exception of £5,000 which has been outstanding for over 90 days. Ways in which the account might be managed in the future include:

- Settlement of the £5,000 due over 90 days. This possibly relates to a single item, on which there may be a customer query outstanding.

- Find ways of selling more goods to this customer.

- Develop better ways of managing customer queries.

Hooper-bikes Limited

Hooper-bikes enjoys a medium sized credit limit from our company, which it has abused in recent months. Also it has exceeded its credit limit and urgent action needs to be taken to bring this account to order. Future action should include the following.

- Ensuring Hooper-bikes reduces outstanding amounts below the available credit limit.

- Considering reducing the credit limit.

- Considering ways of improving Hooper-bikes' payment record.

- Considering reducing sales to Hooper-bikes.

Dynamo Cycles Limited

Dynamo Cycles enjoys only a modest credit limit from our company and has a good payment record. In the future we could consider the following.

- Increasing sales to Dynamo.

- Increasing Dynamo Cycles' credit limit.

Activity 5

Answer C ✓

Activity 6

Answer A ✓

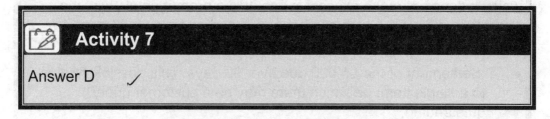

Activity 7

Answer D ✓

KAPLAN PUBLISHING

12 Test your knowledge

 Workbook Activity 8

Task 1

An extract from EKAT's aged trade receivable analysis as at 30 April 20X7 is shown on the next page, followed by a proforma aged trade receivable analysis for May. You should assume the date is 3 June 20X7. Use the information below on transactions which took place during May to complete the May aged trade receivable analysis.

Customer	Information
Gartcosh	Paid invoice K449 £9,000.
	Invoice K496 remains unpaid.
	Invoice K521 £5,000 issued.
Strathaven	Paid invoice K495 £7,000.
	Invoice K511 £6,600 issued.
Coatbridge	Paid invoice K323 £3,000.
	Invoice K411 remains unpaid.
	Invoice K502 £2,775 issued.
New Mains	Invoices K289 £8,000 and K487 £2,000 remain unpaid.
	Invoice K508 £4,000 issued.
Castlemilk	Paid invoice K442 £4,000.
	Invoice K472 £11,000 remains unpaid.
Rutherglen	Invoice K481 £1,000 remains unpaid.
Cambuslang	Invoice K204 £1,500 remains unpaid.
Easterhouse	Paid invoice K331 £10,000.
	Invoice K392 £13,000 remains unpaid.
	Invoice K510 £3,000 issued.
Airdrie	Paid half invoice K234, balance remains unpaid.
Stewartfield	Paid invoice K382 £3,000.
	Invoice K513 £5,000 issued.

EKAT Aged Trade receivables Analysis – 30 April 20X7. Credit terms: 30 days

Customer name and ref	Total amount	Invoice not yet due	Outstanding 1 month	Outstanding 2 months	Outstanding 3 months	Outstanding > 3 months	Action 1 Statement 2 1st reminder 3 2nd reminder 4 Telephone call 5 Warning letter 6 Recovery action implemented					
							1	2	3	4	5	6
Gartcosh	£14,000		£5,000 K496	£9,000 K449			03-Mar K449 03-Apr K496	03-Apr K449				
Strathaven	£7,000		£7,000 K495				03-Apr K495					
Coatbridge	£6,000			£3,000 K411	£3,000 K323		03-Feb K323 03-Mar K422	03-Mar K323 03-Apr K411				
New Mains	£10,000		£2,000 K487			£8,000 K289	03-Jan K289 03-Apr K487	03-Feb K289	03-Mar K289	03-Apr K289		
Castlemilk	£15,000		£11,000 K472	£4,000 K442			03-Mar K442 03-Apr K472	03-Apr K442				
Rutherglen	£1,000		£1,000 K481				03-Apr K481					
Cambuslang	£1,500					£1,500 K204	03-Dec K204	03-Jan K204	03-Feb K204	03 Mar K204	03-Apr K204	
Easterhouse	£23,000		£13,000 K392	£10,000 K331			03-Feb K331 03-Apr K392	03-Mar K331				
Airdrie	£5,500				£5,500 K234		03-Feb K234	03-Mar K234	03-Apr K234			
Stewartfield	£3,000			£3,000 K382			03-Mar K382	03-Apr K382				
TOTALS	£86,000		£39,000	£29,000	£8,500	£9,500						

EKAT Aged Trade receivables Analysis – 30 April 20X7. Credit terms: 30 days

Customer name and ref	Total amount	Invoice not yet due	Outstanding 1 month	Outstanding 2 months	Outstanding 3 months	Outstanding > 3 months	Action 1	2	3	4	5	6
Gartcosh	£10000	£5000 K54	£5000 K521	£5000 K496				03-May K496				
Strathaven	£6600	£6600 K511	K2									
Coatbridge	£5775	£2775 K502			£3000 K411				03-May K411			
New Mains	£14000	£4000 K508		£2000 KU81		£8000 K289		03-May K489			03-May K289	
Castlemilk	£11900			£11000 K472					03 May K442			
Rutherglen	£1000			£1000 KU81				03-May KU81				
Cambuslang	£1500				£1500 K204							03-May K204
Easterhouse	£16000	£3000 K510		£13000 K392		03-May K392						
Airdrie	£2750				£2750 K294					03-May K294		
Stewartfield	£5000	£5000 K513										
TOTALS	£73125		£5000	£31000	£3000	£11250						

Task 2

For each customer, outline briefly how that account should be managed.

- Gartcosh   a medium-sized, regular customer
- Coatbridge   a large, major customer
- New Mains   a medium-sized, regular customer
- Cambuslang   a small and irregular customer
- Airdrie   a large and irregular customer

Workbook Activity 9

Debt collection policy for Green Ltd is as follows:

(i)   Invoices are issued at time of delivery

(ii)   Statements are sent monthly

(iii)   Terms are payment within 30 days

(iv)   Aged analysis is produced monthly

(v)   Reminder letter is sent when debt is 14 days overdue

(vi)   At 28 days overdue a telephone call is made and account is put on stop

(vii) At 60 days overdue it is placed in hands of debt collector unless debt is disputed

(viii) At 90 days overdue legal proceedings are started.

Aged analysis of trade receivables at 31st March 2010

Customer	Balance £	Current £	31-60 days £	61-90 days £	Over90 days £
White Ltd	32,000				32,000
Grey Ltd	24,800		24,800		
Brown Ltd	144,000			48,000	96,000

Notes

- White Ltd went into liquidation a little while ago and the statement of affairs shows that there are very few assets

- Grey Ltd is a regular customer and the latest invoice is dated 28th February 2010

- Brown Ltd has historically been a good payer, but there are rumours that the business is currently in trouble due to overtrading

For each of the above, state what action should have been taken to date, and what further action will be taken. State whether any provision should be made in each case

 Workbook Activity 10

Debt collection policy for Purple Ltd is as follows:

(i)   Invoices are issued at time of delivery

(ii)   Terms are payment within 30 days

(iii) Aged analysis is produced monthly

(iv) Reminder telephone call is made when the debt is 7 days overdue

(v)   Overdue letter is sent when debt is 14 days overdue

(vi) At 28 days overdue the account is put on stop

(vii) At 60 days overdue it is placed in hands of debt collector unless debt is disputed or legal proceedings are started

(viii) Purple is credit insured, however insurance is only given for customers once they have a history of trade with the business of at least 12 months and have successfully paid at least 2 invoiced amounts

Aged analysis of trade receivables at 31st October 2010

Customer	Balance £	Current £	31-60 days £	61-90 days £	Over90 days £
Orange Ltd	40,000				40,000
Yellow Ltd	22,500		22,500		
Red Ltd	50,000			24,000	26,000

Notes

- Orange Ltd is a new customer and has said that the goods were not received in good condition. The delivery note states that any claim for poor quality goods has to be notified to Purple Ltd within 24 hours. Orange Limited only raised a problem with the goods when they were called for a second time. They did not mention that the goods were poor quality on the first call or within 24 hours of delivery

- Yellow Ltd is a regular customer and usually pays to terms

- Red Ltd is refusing to pay even though there is no dispute

For each of the above, state what action should have been taken to date, and what further action will be taken. State whether any provision should be made in each case.

WORKBOOK ACTIVITIES
ANSWERS

Workbook activities answers

1 Legislation

Activity 12

No – the additional amount does not have to be paid as the agreement was for £300

Activity 13

Answer A

Activity 14

Answer C, F, A, E, D, B

2 Granting credit

Activity 6

Answer A

Activity 7

Answer C

£4,000 × 97% = £3,880

(3/97) × (365/(45-10)) × 100 = 32.3%

 Activity 8

The bank reference is sufficient but doesn't appear to be too encouraging ('should prove good for your figures'). The first trade reference had offered a £10,000 credit limit for 30 days; the second comes from a customer not a supplier.

There is at present insufficient evidence to grant Crocodile Cuts' request. However, further research should be carried out and possibly a trial period considered where, perhaps offering a lower limit with shorter terms of sale. We can offer to trade with them for cash until they can provide further references/details.

3 Analysis of credit information

Activity 7

Crust Limited	Indicator Current year	Rating	Indicator Previous year	Rating
Operating profit margin	3.4%	0	1.6%	0
Interest cover	26.3	10	17.7	10
Current ratio	2.2	10	1.4	0
Gearing	10%	20	7.3%	20
Total rating		40		30

Workings for Indicators

Indicator	Current year	Previous year
Operating profit margin	105,000/3,100,000 × 100	53,000/3,350,000 × 100
Interest cover	105,000/4,000	53,000/3,000
Current ratio	167,000/77,000	160,000/115,000
Gearing	40,000/(360,000+40,000) × 100	30,000/(382,000+30,000) × 100

Crust Limited is a very low risk for both sets of accounts analysed.

Draft notes for telephone call:

Ensure that conversation is with the relevant person

Confirm that credit will be granted

Request the information to be able to set up a credit account. This includes:

• confirmation of name

- confirmation of address
- VAT registration number

It is also necessary to agree the terms and conditions of the credit agreement i.e. confirm credit terms and credit limit

Other things that would be discussed include:

- if there will be a settlement discount for prompt or early payment
- it will be necessary to agreeing how payment will be made (more detail later in the chapter)

  any legal conditions within the contract such as 'Retention of Title'.

4 Managing trade receivables

Activity 8

Action legend:
1 Statement
2 1st reminder
3 2nd reminder
4 Telephone call
5 Warning letter
6 Recovery action implemented

Customer name and ref	Total amount	Invoice not yet due	Outstanding 1 month	Outstanding 2 months	Outstanding 3 months	Outstanding > 3 months	Action 1	2	3	4	5	6
Gartcosh	£10,000	£5,000 K521		£5,000 K496			03-Apr K496	03-May K496				
Strathaven	£6,600	£6,600 K511										
Coatbridge	£5,775	£2,775 K502			£3,000 K411		03-Mar K411	03-Apr K411	03-May K411			
New Mains	£14,000	£4,000 K508		£2,000 K487		£8,000 K289	03-Jan K289 / 03-Apr K487	03-Feb K289 / 03-May K487	03-Mar K289	03-Apr K289	03-May K289	
Castlemilk	£11,000			£1,000 K472			03-Apr K472	03-May K472				
Rutherglen	£1,000			£1,000 K481			03-Apr K481	03-May K481				
Cambuslang	£1,500					£1,500 K204	03-Dec K204	03-Jan K204	03-Feb K204	03 Mar K204	03-Apr K204	05-May K204

1 2 3 73

Easterhouse	£16,000		£13,000 K392				03-Apr K392	03-May K392			
Airdrie	£2,750					£2,750 K234	03-Feb K234	03-Mar K234	03-Apr K234	03-May K234	
Stewartfield	£5,000	£5,000 K513					03-Mar K382	03-Apr K382			
TOTALS	£73,625	£26,375		£32,000	£2,000	£12,250					

Task 2

Gartcosh

A good customer that appears to take over 60 days to make payment. Consider ways of encouraging prompt payment, e.g. settlement discounts.

Coatbridge

A large customer seemingly abusing their credit terms at the expense of a small supplier (EKAT). Consider ways of improving relationship and obtaining prompt payment, e.g. provision of settlement discount.

New Mains

A particular problem seems to exist with invoice K289, and invoice K487 is outstanding for two months. Establish whether a query exists with the invoice regarding quality or service. If there are no problems, consider ways of enforcing payment, using the legal process or a debt collection agency.

Cambuslang

A small customer with one outstanding invoice (K204). Establish whether this is in dispute. If not enforce payment using the legal process or a debt collection agency. Be prepared to write-off the debt.

Airdrie

Establish why K234 has been part-paid. Investigate why action has not been taken to recover this earlier. Negotiate with Airdrie for full payment.

Activity 9

Debtor	Completed action	Further action
White	All action should have been taken	As unsecured debtors are low down the list when paying in a case of liquidation – write off the debt (Bad debt)
Grey	Should have received invoice and statement	No further action required at this stage as the debt is not yet 14 days overdue
Brown	Both amounts should have been placed in the hands of a debt collector. Legal proceeding should have started for the £96,000 debt	Provision for doubtful debt as there is doubt over whether the company is going to be able to keep trading

Activity 10

Debtor	Completed action	Further action
Orange	All above action should have been taken	Orange is in breach of contract as they had not contacted Purple within the agreed timescales. Purple can take Orange to court to seek action for damages etc. It is not possible to use the credit insurance as Orange is a new customer. Provision should be made.
Yellow	Invoice and statement should have been sent	Reminder telephone call may be required depending on the date of the invoice
Red	All above action should have been taken	Both debts need to be placed in the hands of the debt collector – there is no dispute. Credit insurance may be possible but more detail is required about length of trading. Provision should be made.

MOCK ASSESSMENT

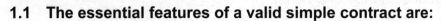

1 Mock Assessment Questions

Section 1 (allow 1 hour)

1.1 The essential features of a valid simple contract are:

A Offer, acceptance and consideration only

B Offer, acceptance, consideration, intention to create legal relations and certainty of terms only

C Offer and acceptance only

D Offer, acceptance, intention to create legal relations only

1.2 Consideration is:

A The intention of the parties to be legally bound

B The need for fairness in the contract

C The promise to exchange value

D The payment of cash

1.3 Steve orders a takeaway by telephone, and says he will pay on delivery. Which of the following would constitute consideration?

A Calling the restaurant

B Handing over money to the delivery person

C Accepting delivery of the takeaway

D Promising to pay for the takeaway

1.4 Bill shops at a supermarket. A contract is formed when:

A Bill pays for his shopping

B Bill puts his selection in the trolley

C The checkout assistant takes Bill's goods

D Bill picks up items from the shelves

1.5 Tina is the owner of a florist. She places a notice in the window advertising the sale of roses at half price. The notice is:

  A   A contractual offer

  B   A completed contract

  C   An acceptance of an offer

  ✓ D   An invitation to treat

1.6 Banana Limited receives a letter from Carrot Limited containing an order for 100 kilograms of rice. Banana sends Carrot a schedule of standard conditions which includes the clause that payment is due within 30 days of invoice date. This clause is an example of:

  A   An invitation to treat

  B   Consideration

  ✓ C   An offer

  D   A misrepresentation

1.7 Jack receives a letter from Mark containing an order of 50kg of sugar for £100. Which of the following statements is correct?

  A   Mark's letter is an invitation to treat and Jack's response that he can supply the sugar is an offer

  ✓ B   Mark's letter is an offer and Jack's response that he can supply the sugar is an acceptance

  C   Mark's letter is an acceptance and Jack's response that he cannot supply the sugar is a breach of contract

  D   Mark's letter is an acceptance and Jack's response that he can supply the sugar is consideration

1.8 Maud orders some clothing which is advertised as being 100% pure new wool. When she receives the goods, the label says 60% wool and 40% Polyester. Maud has a claim for breach of contract due to:

  A   Fiduciary misconduct

  ✓ A   Misrepresentation

  B   Misuse of Sales Act

  C   Unfair Contract Terms Act

1.9 The Late Payment of Commercial Debts (Interest) Act allows:

A   Customers to charge interest on overdue amounts owing

B   Commercial banks to charge interest on loans

✓C   Suppliers to charge interest on overdue amounts owing

D   Suppliers to give discounts for early payment

1.10 Nikki asks Harold for a price to paint the interior of her flat. Harold says he can do it for £200 and Nikki says that will be fine. Halfway through the work Harold asks for an additional sum of £100 because he underestimated the work. Which of the following statements are correct?

A   Nikki must pay Harold the £100 because the agreement was made in good faith and Harold made a mistake

✓B   Harold cannot force Nikki to pay the additional amount because the agreement was for £200

C   Harold can force Nikki to pay because she never accepted the price

D   If Nikki refuses to pay Harold can simply work until he has done £200 worth of painting

2.1 The Data Protection Act applies to:

✓A   Data about individuals only

B   Data about individuals, companies and government departments

C   Data about companies only

D   Data about individuals and companies only

2.2 The Data Protection Act applies to:

✓A   All records held by the company

B   Only manual records

C   Only computer records

D   Only records of opinions

3.1 **Company Banana has a customer, Carrot limited, who refuses to pay an outstanding amount of £500. Which of the following courts will deal with any action taken by Banana to enforce the repayment of the debt?**

A The High Court

B An Industrial Tribunal

C A Small Claims Court

D The County Court

3.2 **Legal action can be taken against a customer for non payment of an invoice when:**

A There is a contract in existence and the non payment is a breach of contract

B There is no contract in existence but the payment is still due

C There is a contract in existence and the non payment is a misrepresentation

D There is a contract in existence and the non payment is a remedy

3.3 **The normal remedy for breach of contract due to non payment of the debt is:**

A An action for specific performance

B An action for price

C An action for remedy

D An action for the goods

3.4 **Retention of title is:**

A The right of the purchaser to retain ownership of the goods received

B The right of the seller to retain ownership of the goods until a cheque has been posted

C The right of the seller to retain ownership of the goods until payment is made

D The right of the purchaser to expect that title is retained by the seller even when payment has been received

KAPLAN PUBLISHING

3.5 In order to petition the court for a winding up order, the company must be owed at least:

A £75

B £750

C £7,500

D £1,000

4.1 Why is liquidity management important?

A Liquidity management is important to ensure that a company does not make a loss

B Liquidity management is important so that the shareholders can see how much return they will get on their investment

C Liquidity management is important so that the company can estimate how much cash is tied up in stock and fixed assets

D Liquidity management is important so that the company can ensure that cash is available to discharge commitments

4.2 Banana Limited has sold goods on credit to Carrot Limited. The following information is available.

(i) Aged trade receivable analysis
(ii) Copies of outstanding invoices
(iii) Copies of contractual documents
(iv) Copies of trade references
(v) Copies of bank references

Which of the above documents will be needed to aid the collection of the outstanding amounts owed by Carrot Limited?

A All items

B (i), (ii) and (iii) only

C (i), (iv) and (v) only

D (iv) and (v) only

4.3 Which of the following information could be used to assess the credit status of a new customer?

(i) Financial accounts
(ii) Aged trade receivable analysis
(iii) Copies of outstanding invoices

(iv) Draft contract for trade

(v) Trade references

(vi) Bank references

A All items

B (i), (ii) and (iii) only

C (i), (iv) and (v) only

✓ D (i), (v) and (vi) only

4.4 Which if the following is not a method of analysing credit control information?

A ✓ Aged payables analysis

B Trading history

C 80/20 rule

D Materiality

4.5 The 80/20 rule method of analysing information on debtors is:

A A rule where you only look at the first 80 customer records

B A rule that 20 customers out of every 100 will go into liquidation

C ✓ A rule that approximately 80% of the value of the amounts owed will be represented by approximately 20% of the customer accounts.

D A rule that the company must make at least 20% profit out of every £100 of goods sold.

5.1 Which of the following is a reason for offering discounts for prompt payment?

A To make the customer feel that they have received a bargain

B ✓ To improve the cash flow of a business

C To make more profit

D To decrease the cost of loans

5.2 **A company's terms of payment are 30 days. It is offering a discount of 4% for payment within 15 days. Customer A owes £2,000. Calculate the amount A will pay if they take advantage of the discount and also the simple annual interest rate of the discount.**

A   £1,920 and 58.402%

B   £1,920 and 97.33%

C   £1,920 and 101.39%

D   £1,920 and 17.12%

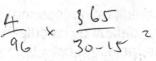

6.1 **Invoice discounting is a method where:**

A   Discounts are given for early payment of invoices

B   A finance house lends money against invoices issued

C   A reduction is given for faulty goods

D   A judgement given by a court

6.2 **Credit insurance allows a company to claim for:**

A   Amounts owed by a customer who has defaulted on payment

B   Amounts owed to a bank on a mortgage

C   Amounts owed to creditors when a company makes losses

D   Amounts owed to shareholders when a director has acted illegally

6.3 **Organisations often use debt collection agencies because:**

A   Debt collection agencies have more powers than ordinary companies

B   Debt collection agencies can place customers on stop with all other suppliers in the sector

C   Debt collection agencies have a right to seize goods from customer

D   Debt collection agencies get results because customers take more notice and are more likely to pay

Section 2 – Project (allow 2 hours)

(a) You work as a credit control manager for Lamb Limited which uses a credit rating system to assess the credit status of new and existing customers.

The credit rating (scoring) system table below is used to assess the risk of default by calculating key indicators (ratios), comparing them to the table and calculating an aggregate score.

Credit rating (scoring) system	Score
Operating profit margin	
Losses	–5
Less than 5%	0
5% and above but less than 10%	5
10% and above but less than 20%	10
More than 20%	20
Interest cover	
No cover	–30
Less than 1	–20
More than 1 but less than 2	–10
More than 2 but less than 4	0
More than 4	10
Liquidity ratio	
Less than 1	–20
Between 1 and 1.25	–10
Between 1.25 and 1.5	0
Above 1.5	10
Gearing (total debt/(total debt plus equity))	
Less than 25%	20
25% and above but less than 50%	10

More than 50% less than 65%	0
Between 65% and 75%	−20
Between 75% and 80%	−40
Above 80%	−100
Risk	Aggregate score
Very low risk	Between 60 and 21
Low risk	Between 20 and 1
Medium risk	Between 0 and −24
High risk	Between −25 and −50
Very high risk	Above −50

New customer request form

The sales department has asked for a credit limit of £50,000 to be given to Cow Limited who is a potential new customer. The financial information below has been supplied by Cow Limited

Accounts for Cow Limited	2009	2010
	£'000	£'000
Turnover	4,500	5,500
Cost of sales	3,500	3,800
Gross profit	1,000	1,700
Distribution costs	1,050	1,150
Administration costs	1,000	1,000
Operating profit	−1,050	−450
Interest payable	100	50
Profit on ordinary activities before taxation	−1,150	−500
Tax on profit on ordinary activities	0	0
Profit for the financial year	−1,150	−500

Statement of financial position	2009	2010
	£'000	**£'000**
Non-current assets		
Tangible assets	2,200	2,500
Current assets		
Inventory	900	750
Trade receivables	1,000	850
Cash	50	400
	1,950	2,000
Payables amounts falling due within one year		
Trade payables	2,100	1,800
Net current assets	−150	200
Payables amounts falling due after more than one year		
Long term loans	1,000	500
Net assets	1,050	2,200
Capital and reserves		
Share capital	200	200
Retained earnings	850	2,000
Shareholders' funds	1,050	2,200

New customer request form

The sales department has asked for a credit limit of £30,000 to be given to Pig Limited who is a potential new customer. The financial information below has been supplied by Pig Limited

Accounts for Pig limited	2009	2010
	£'000	£'000
Turnover	9,000	8,000
Cost of sales	6,250	6,000
Gross profit	2,750	2,000
Distribution costs	850	850
Administration costs	600	600
Operating profit	1,300	550
Interest payable	250	250
Profit on ordinary activities before taxation	1,050	300
Tax on profit on ordinary activities	350	100
Profit for the financial year	700	200
Statement of financial position	**2009**	**2010**
	£'000	£'000
Non-current assets		
Tangible assets	4,500	3,900
Current assets		
Inventory	1,200	1,000
Trade receivables	700	600
Cash	400	400
	2,300	2,000

Payables amounts falling due within one year		
Trade payables	1,500	1,300
Net current assets	800	700
Payables amounts falling due after more than one year		
Long term loans	2,500	2,500
Net assets	2,800	2,100
Capital and reserves		
Share capital	100	100
Retained earnings	2,700	2000
Shareholders' funds	2,800	2,100

1.1 Using the templates provided:

(i)   Calculate the key indicators for 2009 and 2010 for Cow Limited and Pig Limited, and

(ii) Rate each company using the credit rating (scoring) system.

Cow Limited	Indicator	Rating	Indicator	Rating
Year	**2009**		**2010**	
Operating profit margin	-23.3%	-5	-8.2%	-5
Interest cover	-6.50	-30	~10	-30
Current ratio	0.53	-20	1.11	-10
Gearing	47.2% 3%	10	56.5% 27.5%	20
		-45		-25

Pig Limited	Indicator	Rating	Indicator	Rating
Year	2009		2010	
Operating profit margin	14.4%	10	6.9%	5
Interest cover	5.2	10	2.2	0
Current ratio	1.53	10	1.54	10
Gearing	47.2%	10	54.3%	0
		40		15

1.2 Based on the results of your credit rating, recommend, with reasons, whether the requested credit limits should be given to Cow Limited and Pig Limited.

1.3 Where credit is being refused, draft a note or a letter communicating the decision and explaining what action the company could take to improve its chances of being granted credit in the future.

OR

Prepare a telephone script which could be used by the person contacting the company to communicate the decision regarding the requested credit limit.

pp 94, 95

pp 90, 91

Existing customer requesting increased credit limit.

Chicken Limited has been trading with Lamb Limited for several years and has, until recently, always paid to terms. Following several late payments they have now contacted Lamb Limited to request an increase in their credit limit from £50,000 to £100,000. Chicken Limited has supplied the accounts below.

Accounts for Chicken Limited	2009	2010
	£'000	£'000
Turnover	6,500	6,000
Cost of sales	4,600	3,800
Gross profit	1,900	2,200
Distribution costs	850	850
Administration costs	600	600
Operating profit	450	750
Interest payable	500	250
Profit on ordinary activities before taxation	−50	500
Tax on profit on ordinary activities	0	150
Profit for the financial year	−50	350

Statement of financial position	2009	2010
	£'000	£'000
Non-current assets		
Tangible assets	7,050	4,350
Current Assets		
Inventory	1,200	550
Trade Receivables	1,300	800
Cash	100	300
	2,600	1,650

Payables amounts falling due within one year		
Trade payables	2,100	1,400
Net current assets	500	250
Payables amounts falling due after more than one year		
Long term loans	5,000	2,000
Net assets	2,550	2,600
Capital and reserves		
Share capital	100	100
Retained earnings	2,450	2,500
Shareholders' funds	2,550	2,600

Additional information supplied by the sales department after a visit to Chicken Limited:

Chicken Limited has recently acquired several new large customers and therefore purchased new assets with long term loans to ensure that forecast sales demands can be met. The contracts with the new customers were only completed in the second half of the year, and it is expected that sales will continue to increase in 2010 with little increase in costs because the new machines have resulted in a reduction in variable cost per unit. The directors of Chicken Limited expect a profit after tax in 2011 of around £500,000. In anticipation of orders for 2011, Chicken Limited significantly increased its inventory levels at the end of 2010.

Required

1.4 Using the templates provided:

(i) Calculate the key indicators for 2009 and 2010 for Chicken Limited, and

(ii) Rate the company using the credit rating (scoring) system.

Chicken Limited	Indicator	Rating	Indicator	Rating
Year	2009		2010	
Operating profit margin	12.5%	10	6.92%	5
Interest cover	3	0	0.9	20
Current ratio	1.18	10	1.24	10
Gearing	43.48%	10	66.23%	20
		10		45

1.5 **Based on the results of your credit rating, and taking into account the trading history and additional information supplied by the sales department, recommend a course of action.**

You could make use of additional terms in the contract or any other options open to Lamb Limited which could provide additional comfort.

(b) You have been provided with the credit control policy for Lamb Limited, and an aged receivable's analysis at 31 March 2010.

Credit control policy for Lamb Limited.

Current credit control procedures once credit limit has been agreed:

1. An order for goods is received by email, fax or phone (all phone calls are recorded).

2. Goods are delivered and a goods received note is signed by the customer.

3. The goods received notes are kept in a file in the accounts office.

4. An invoice will be issued a few days after delivery on 30 day terms.

5. An aged analysis of trade debtors is produced monthly.

6. A reminder telephone call is made when the debt is 7 days overdue.

7. When a debt is 14 days overdue a letter is sent.

8. When the account is 28 days overdue the account will be put on stop.

9. The debt will either be placed in the hands of a debt collection company or legal proceedings could be instigated if the customer does not respond to calls or letters.

10. The business is credit insured, however insurance is only given for customers once they have a history of trade with the business of at least 12 months and have successfully paid for at least 3 invoiced amounts.

Aged receivables analysis as at 30 September 2010

Customer	Balance £	0 – 30 days £	31 – 60 days £	61 – 90 days £	Over 90 days £
Pink	10,000	10,000			
Blue	25,000			25,000	
Green	60,000	30,000	30,000		
White	35,000	10,000	10,000	15,000	
Brown	60,000	60,000			
Cerise	25,000	5,000	20,000		
Red	10,000	(50,000)	10,000		50,000
Yellow	25,000				25,000
Violet	33,000	33,000			
Amber	20,000			20,000	
Mauve	120,000	30,000	30,000	30,000	30,000
Beige	40,000	20,000	20,000		
Taupe	99,200		44,200	55,000	
Auburn	100,000			100,000	
Russet	3,000				3,000
Black	6,000			6,000	

The assistant responsible for credit control has been on sick leave for several months but you have access to notes she prepared.

Notes provided by the assistant credit controller

A. Pink is a new customer and placed its first order a few weeks ago.

No action
Visit Blue to try to resolve dispute

B. Blue have said that they placed an order for a particular grade of product but received a different product and are therefore not prepared to pay the invoice.

Put a stop on account

C. Green is a new customer and has said that a cheque is in the post. There is a rumour circulating that the company is having financial problems and has not been paying its suppliers. Green has placed an order for £10,000 of goods.

D. White has a history of paying late but they have always paid eventually

No action

E. Brown is a long standing customer and has always settled their account within trading terms.

Contact the Administrator

F. Cerise has gone into administration. The account is not credit insured.

Phone red for confirmation –

G. Red sent a payment of £50,000 but did not provide details of which invoices the payment relates to.

Place collection of debt with credit collection agency

H. Yellow is a new customer and has said that the goods were not received in good condition. The delivery note states that any claim for poor quality goods has to be notified to Lamb Limited within 24 hours. Yellow only raised a problem with the goods when they were called for the second time. They did not mention that the goods were poor quality on the first call or within 24 hours of delivery.

Place collection of debt with debt collection agency

I. Violet is a new customer and has only placed the one order. They have not responded to any correspondence and the letter was returned stating the company had gone away.

debt collection (legal agency proceedings)

J. Amber is a new business and traded on cash with order. The assistant credit controller allowed the order to be processed before the cheque had cleared. The cheque subsequently bounced and the company is not returning calls.

Set up meeting between Directors of Mauve and Lamb
Put stop on account

K. Mauve is a long established customer and has always paid eventually, but has a history of late payments. The Managing Director of Mauve is a personal friend of Lamb Limited's Managing Director.

L. Beige has been purchasing £20,000 per month

legal proceedings

M. Taupe is a regular customer and normally pays but payment can take several months – usually once a notice of intention to start legal proceedings in issued.

Contact credit insurer and Administrator

N. Auburn has recently gone into liquidation. Auburn had been a customer for 5 years and the account is credit insured.

legal proceedings O. Russet is an individual customer who is refusing to pay even though there is no dispute.

legal proceedings P. Black keeps saying that the cheque is in the post.

Required

Review the aged receivables analysis and the assistant's notes and prepare an action plan. The action plan should include a summary of options available for the company to pursue and recommendations for provisions or write off of bad debts where appropriate.

2 Mock Assessment Answers

Section 1

1.1 **A** Offer, acceptance, consideration, intention to create legal relations and certainty of terms only

1.2 **C** The promise to exchange value

1.3 **D** Promising to pay for the pizza

1.4 **C** The checkout assistant takes Dave's goods

1.5 **D** An invitation to treat

1.6 **B** Consideration

1.7 **B** Michael's letter is an offer and John's response that he can supply the sugar is an acceptance

1.8 **B** Misrepresentation

1.9 **C** Suppliers to charge interest on overdue amounts owing

1.10 **B** Harry cannot force Nita to pay the additional amount because the agreement was for £200.

2.1 **A** Data about individuals only

2.2 **A** All records held by the company

3.1 **C** A Small Claims Court

3.2 **A** There is a contract in existence and the non payment is a breach of contract

3.3 **B** An action for price

3.4 **C** The right of the seller to retain ownership of the goods until payment is made

3.5 **B** £750

4.1 **D**   Liquidity management is important so that the company can ensure that cash is available to discharge commitments

4.2 **B**   i), ii) and iii) only

4.3 **D**   i), v) and vi) only

4.4 **A**   Aged creditor analysis

4.5 **C**   A rule that approximately 80% of the value of the amounts owed will be represented by approximately 20% of the customer accounts

5.1 **B**   To improve the cash flow of a business

5.2 **C**   £1,920, and 101.33%

6.1 **B**   A finance house lends money against invoices issued

6.2 **A**   Amounts owed by a customer who has defaulted on payment

6.3 **D**   Debt collection agencies get results because customers take more notice and are more likely to pay

Section 2

(a)

Cow and Pig Limited

Cow Limited	Indicator	Rating	Indicator	Rating
Year	2009		2010	
Operating profit margin	−23.33%	−5	−8.18%	−5
Interest cover	0	−30	0	−30
Current ratio	0.93	−20	1.11	−10
Gearing	48.78%	10	18.52%	20
		−45		−25

Pig Limited	Indicator	Rating	Indicator	Rating
Year	2009		2010	
Operating profit margin	14.44%	10	6.88%	5
Interest cover	5.2	10	2.2	0
Current ratio	1.53	10	1.54	10
Gearing	47.17%	10	54.35%	0
		40		15

Cow Limited achieves a high risk credit score and should therefore be turned down for a credit limit. A letter/note should be drafted explaining in a polite way the reasons for refusal of credit, and what the company could do to improve its chances of getting credit in future.

Pig Limited achieved a low risk and therefore credit can be given.

Chicken Limited

	Indicator	Rating	Indicator	Rating
Year	**2009**		**2010**	
Operating profit margin	6.92%	5	12.50%	10
Interest cover	0.9	–20	3	0
Current ratio	1.24	–10	1.18	–10
Gearing	66.23	–20	43.48%	10
		–45		10

The above table shows that Chicken Limited's credit rating has reduced substantially and is now rated as a high risk. However, there are certain factors in its favour. These include:

- A good trading history over several years, although recently they have made some late payments.

- The expansion plan and the fact that the bank has given loans for the purchase of new assets is a good sign.

- New customers have ordered goods and have indicated that they will continue in 2011.

- The company is still liquid with cash at bank at the year end.

It is worth considering taking some kind of security over the business or personal guarantees from the directors or to consider retention of title clauses. There is no right decision and as long as the credit controller considers all the issues and makes a reasoned decision, credit will be awarded.

(b)

A reasoned argument for each overdue account and recommendation of actions and provisions is required.

Pink – no action needed

Blue – Lamb Limited needs to check sales order and delivery note. Arrange for wrong delivery to be collected and new delivery sent if at fault.

Green – is already at its credit limit so no more orders should be processed until the payment is received.

White – has a debt of £35,000 which is within their limit. They usually take 90 days to settle. A chasing letter should be sent and the account should be on stop. A telephone call maybe needed to discuss credit terms. A cash discount could be offered to encourage early payment

Brown – no action needed

Cerise – there is no credit insurance so no claim can be made. Lamb Limited should contact the administrator for retention of title and any dividend. The £25,000 debt should be written off the VAT claimed back

Red – a telephone call is needed to confirm which invoice the payment is against

Yellow - Under the terms and conditions any fault should have been notified to Lamb Limited within 48 hours of receipt. The account should be placed on stop and Yellow should be notified that legal proceeding will be started if payment is not received. A provision for the debt should be made.

Violet – a telephone call is required to check postal details. A provision for the debt should be provided as there is uncertainty.

Amber – Lamb Limited needs to investigate how this could happen. The credit controller responsible for this needs to been spoken to. Telephone calls need to be made to locate Amber and chase for payment. Legal proceedings may be started if necessary. A provision should be provided at this stage, a write off may be necessary

Mauve – Lamb Limited's MD should have a chat with Mauve's MD as usually credit control lines have not succeeded. Account may be put on stop until this conversation has been had.

Beige - is already at its credit limit so no more orders should be processed until the payment is received

Taupe – account should be put on stop and credit terms revised

Auburn – the insurance company should be contacted to regain the debt

Russet – legal proceedings should be started and the account should be put on stop. A provision for the debt should be made

Black – Lamb Limited should ask about the cheque number, when it was sent, what address it was sent to and the value of the cheque. Account should be put on stop until payment is received. Suggest that a new cheque is issued with a new deadline date. Legal action should be taken if the cheque is still not received. A provision for the debt should be made.

INDEX

KAPLAN PUBLISHING